PROGRAMME

BY ROYAL COMMAND

BY ROYAL COMMAND

BILL PERTWEE

DAVID & CHARLES

Newton Abbot   London   North Pomfret (Vt)

British Library Cataloguing in Publication Data

Pertwee, Bill
  By royal command
  1. Performing arts
  2. Great Britain – Kings and rulers
  I. Title
  790.2' 098   PN1581

ISBN 0–7153–8200–4

Typeset by Typesetters (Birmingham) Ltd, Smethwick, Warley
and printed in Great Britain
by Ebenezer Baylis and Son, Limited,
The Trinity Press, Worcester, and London
for David & Charles (Publishers) Limited
Brunel House   Newton Abbot   Devon

Published in the United States of America
by David & Charles Inc
North Pomfret   Vermont 05053 USA

FOREWORD

I know Bill Pertwee personally, and millions more through stage, TV and radio will know him as a busy and gifted comedy actor and entertainer. For a variety of reasons I am delighted to welcome his book, in particular because I have the honour to be Life President of the Entertainment Artistes Benevolent Fund and part of the proceeds will be going to that worthy charity which helps to make life easier for aged artistes who have fallen on difficult times.

Royal shows are something I do know about. I presented the annual Royal Variety Performance for twenty-one years from 1958 — and altogether I have been responsible for more than thirty similar occasions. You would think that putting them together grows easier. It doesn't. The wear and tear, stress and strain grow worse. After such a gala night it is like being in a car crash and walking away badly shocked. I still get the shivers remembering the problems of getting these shows to run to time. You are presenting some of the world's greatest stars who are appearing unpaid for charity. How can you call a halt if for whatever reason they decide to stay on stage?

In fact, of course, the real stars of any of these glittering occasions are the Royal Family. They are the reason the top artistes appear and why millions of pounds have been raised for charity. I know exactly what it means for show business performers to be invited to appear before the Queen. For years I was on stage myself as part of the Delfont Boys dance act. We were invariably first on the bill and it was always my ambition to be selected for the Royal Variety Performance. I knew deep down that accolade would never come to me, but if I had been told that for two decades I would have the honour and responsibility of actually presenting the Royal Performance, I would never have believed it.

I shall never forget my first experience of assembling a Royal show. I was so nervous I was unable to sit down and watch. So I stood outside the swing doors and listened to the applause. As he left the Duke of Edinburgh told me: 'You look haggard. Go and have a good week's sleep.' They are inevitably wonderful, nervous, electric, traumatic, and unforgettable evenings for the profession and public alike.

I am glad to have played some part and congratulate Mr Pertwee on his billing of the story of the royal 'commands' over the centuries. It is a fascinating account and explains how the palaces of entertainment throughout the land have become that much closer to another palace at the end of The Mall.

CONTENTS

Awaiting the arrival of the Royal Party outside the Palladium. *Photograph Doug McKenzie, PPS*

It is a misty evening in November and already the last shoppers and office girls are making their way homewards, soon to be swallowed up in the darkness of Oxford Circus where taxis, buses and Tube trains will transport them away from the metropolis to main line stations on their journey to suburbia and, for the majority of them, another evening of normality.

The fruit stall on the corner of Argyll Street has been 'moved on' for the evening, its attendant stallholder happy to co-operate with the police on this particular occasion. The last vestige of banana skin and squashed orange tidied away, little knots of people begin to gather on the pavement's edge outside the London Palladium and its immediate surrounds — an air of expectancy quietly manifesting itself.

Within a short time the crowds will swell and those at the back will be standing permanently on tiptoe. The familiar cry, 'Here they are' will be heard as the dark shape of the royal car, with its bonnet flags fluttering, comes silently into view. Before the car has stopped an aide is already out of the door walking with the car to its final, carefully planned, prearranged stopping place. As the royal party alight, white gloves wave a greeting to onlookers, and diamonds and smiles sparkle in the light of the photographers' flash bulbs — the results of which will be seen in the next morning's dailies. At this point the television presentation of the Royal Command Variety Performance has been under way for some minutes, setting the scene that will be viewed by millions — not only in this country but throughout the world.

Lord Delfont, who has greeted the royal party at the Palladium Royal Command Variety performances for 21 years (in his capacity as producer of the show) moves forward on the steps of this great theatre to greet Her Majesty the Queen, HRH Prince Philip and other members of the Royal Family. With Lord Delfont are other dignitaries connected with the theatrical profession, among them Reg Swinson, Secretary of the Entertainment Artistes Benevolent Fund, the fund devoted to helping performers or their families who may be sick, aged or fallen on hard times. As a result of this one performance the funds will be increased by many thousands of pounds and once again the less fortunate will benefit. A very large amount of the money raised each year goes to the upkeep of Brinsworth House and the welfare of its residents.

Inside the foyer of the theatre, the atmosphere is electric: the welcoming party — now swelled by members of the Palladium staff and personnel of the EABF Committee — all rejoicing in this night that is as much theirs as anybody's. Introductions to the Royal Family are made, a word here, a smile there, more camera flashes. The honour of presenting a bouquet to Her Majesty is accorded to someone special on this night — it may be one of the elderly residents of Brinsworth who will step forward at the given time for the presentation. It is now time to move on and into the Royal Box, which has been bedecked with the most beautiful flowers, carefully chosen to blend with the colour of Her Majesty's gown. It is now that any small last-minute queries or requests are discussed between Lord Delfont and the royal party.

Inside the auditorium the air is heavy with expensive perfume and the minks and sables are out in force. The atmosphere of excitement and anticipation mounts as the vast audience await the final spark that will ignite the proceedings. The Musical Director raises his baton on cue as the royal party enter the 'Box' and, as one, the audience rivet their gaze on the small figure whose presence makes this night a magical one for everyone concerned. The National Anthem is played by the orchestra as they've seldom played it before. When it ends the applause breaks out in spontaneous affection and, perhaps, relief that another royal performance is about to start.

1
OVERTURE AND BEGINNERS

It is quite natural that the royal performance should be thought of in terms of fairly recent theatrical history. This certainly is not the case, and perhaps the first conscious Command Performance may have been before King Herod in biblical times, with Salome doing her stuff.

Most of the medieval kings had their own jesters or minstrels who at a 'royal command' would caper or play their musical instruments at one end of the hall where the King and his court were dining. There was a jester in practically every important household in the early Middle Ages, who often became a faithful and loyal friend to the family: Galet, Blondel and Rahere were all faithful retainers. Rahere was a jester to Henry I and was a very amusing performer, but having had enough of playing the fool, in later life he became a monk and eventually founded the famous St Bartholomew's Hospital. Henry VIII's fool was one Will Somers, short, almost like a hunchback. A deep friendship developed between the two men: wives and Ministers came and went, but Will stayed.

Henry's daughter Elizabeth I was amongst the first reigning monarchs to command whole entertainments and defended the performers who had become 'her' actors from the attacks of the Puritans. They had accused Her Majesty's company of flaunting it in silks and satins. Whatever would they have said about today's modern drag artistes! Queen Elizabeth's company of a dozen actors who were regularly commanded to Court was headed by Richard Tarleton, who could always make her laugh with his cheeky repartee. Another leading actor popular during the Queen's reign was Richard Burbage, who was the first actor to play Hamlet, Othello, King Lear and Richard III at the Globe Theatre, which had become so closely associated with William Shakespeare. He and Burbage appeared before Elizabeth in a commanded performance at Greenwich Palace in 1594. Shakespeare's *Comedy of Errors* was given its *première* in the presence of Her Majesty, as was *A Midsummer Night's Dream.*

But Elizabeth was not the first reigning monarch to have a company of players; the first was Richard III, and it is ironical that he was to encourage the drama of which he was himself to be the archvillain.

James I of England was very fond of dramatic entertainments, and his commands put a great strain on the privy purse. Both the King and his Queen, Anne of Denmark, favoured masques, and at one given in 1606 for King Christian of Denmark the ladies of the Court were seen to abandon all 'sobriety and roll about in intoxication'. The King encouraged them for he liked watching women being immodest. As far as Shakespeare's comedies were concerned, James enjoyed the low comedy and burlesque in the productions, and royal patronage continued for the Bard.

Charles I had many diverse interests, the theatre amongst them, but his preference was for masques and informal Court entertainment. Both he and his Queen, Henrietta Maria, liked to have dwarfs as their jesters. One of them, Jeffrey Hudson, who was often at Windsor, apparently stood no higher than eighteen inches when he was a young boy. He jumped out of a pie one day on to Her Majesty's dining-table in a miniature suit of armour and bowed politely to the Queen. He grew a little in later years, but remained small enough to fit into the pocket of the King's gigantic porter, whose pretence of eating him as a tasty snack between two halves of a loaf was greatly enjoyed at Court masques. He was eventually knighted by the King.

Kings and queens of England through the ages have always enjoyed and supported the theatre, and commands to Court have at times been taken for granted. The great value of royal patronage was obvious during the reign of the puritanical Oliver Cromwell. With Charles II's defeat and subsequent exile in France, theatres were closed and the actors, nearly all of whom were Royalists, were severely persecuted. Once Charles returned to his throne theatres re-opened, new ones were built, and players and companies were re-formed with gusto and enthusiasm. The King was a lover of the theatre, and one of his first acts on returning to London from exile was to license two new theatres, one at Lincoln's Inn, which became the home of a company headed by actor Sir William Davenant. He had, incidentally, been knighted for bravery on the battle-field during the fighting against Cromwell. His players were known as the Duke's Men. Another company, headed by playwright Thomas Killigrew and called the King's Men, had a theatre designed for them in Drury Lane on the site of the present Theatre Royal. It is a well known fact that Charles II didn't confine his patronage to theatres: his first mistress, Moll Davies, was an actress he met in Tunbridge Wells, although she was soon replaced by Nell Gwynne, who was in fact a fine comedy actress. Samuel Pepys, among others, was annoyed when Nell gave up acting. She became the King's constant companion, remaining faithful to him until he died.

Sir Jeffrey Hudson, who was presented to Charles I and his Queen in a cold pie. *Photograph courtesy of BBC Hulton Picture Library*

The King's porter and dwarf. *Photograph courtesy of BBC Hulton Picture Library*

When Queen Anne came to the throne, she set a different standard. Theatrical performances had become too bawdy for her taste and she felt that most plays during the seventeenth century had been an influence against religion. She commanded performances at Court by special companies that did not offend and on one occasion watched a performance of Dryden's *All for Love* on her birthday.

On February 3rd, 1794, King George III commanded a performance at the Haymarket. A Royal Command in those days, as in these, drew great crowds. The little theatre was besieged and it was clear that only a portion of the waiting crowd would ever get in. There was no queueing then. It was a vast, milling mob round the pit door; the battle (and the seats) was to the strong. The opening of the pit door at any theatre on a big night was always the signal for a free fight, and this February night in 1794 was to be no exception. But alas! It was not to be an occasion of cuts, bruises and faintings, it was to be marked by a real tragedy. The pit doors opened and at once the mob surged forward. A man in the front, pressed by the mob behind him, fell down the stairs. Those following tumbled over him, and in a second or so there was a screaming, struggling heap of humanity being trodden underfoot by the onrushing crowd behind. Fifteen people were trampled to death, nineteen severely injured, and many more slightly hurt.

They did not tell the King and Queen of the disaster, and the show went on. The news was broken to the Royal visitors after they had returned to the Palace. There was no further Royal Command after that at the Haymarket until 1803.[1]

George III and Queen Charlotte loved the theatre, and this was almost entirely due to Sarah Siddons. 'Mrs. Siddons' had failed once at Drury Lane, but after long and substantial provincial tours learning her trade and gaining critical acclaim she was invited back to the city she knew she would one day conquer. This she certainly did. Her first season there was great, but the ensuing one was to add fresh lustre to her reputation. The King and Queen ordered a 'Command Performance', and with the Royal Family, attended in state.

The front of the Royal Box was built out for this occasion, so that His Majesty's subjects might have a chance of feasting their loyal and dazzled eyes on the glory of Royalty. A canopy was extended over the Royal heads. It had a dome of crimson velvet adorned with carved and gilded decorations, and the draping valances were also enriched with cords of gold. Its furniture was almost overpowering in its regal splendour. The Monarch had determined to show his people what he could do when he wished, and for one to whom he wished well. He himself wore a plain quaker coloured suit, although it had gold buttons; but the Queen literally gleamed in white satin and diamonds. One Princess wore a blue and white, and the other a rose and white, dress of figured silk. They had a canopy of their own of blue satin. His Royal

Highness the Prince of Wales (to be the First Gentleman in Europe and the very form and mould of fashion and 'nobility') sat in solitary state under a canopy of blue velvet trimmed with silver, and put his plainly attired father quite in the shade by sporting a suit of dark blue Geneva velvet smothered in gold lace. That is how Royalty went to the show when the show was Siddons.[2]

In the summer of 1788 Sarah was commanded to appear in Brighton before the Prince Regent and Lady Jersey. She enjoyed playing to His Royal Highness but was not very happy on being commanded to have supper with him, as she thoroughly disapproved of the Prince's relationship with Lady Jersey. The Prince enjoyed the theatre and theatre people as much as his father, and may have even fancied himself as a performer — he liked dressing up and certainly had the right figure for pantomime.

Theatre audiences during the latter part of the eighteenth century and beginning of the nineteenth century had become somewhat unruly, and in some instances almost violent. Middle- and upper-class theatre-goers felt fairly safe attending the opera and ballet, knowing there was little chance of anything unpleasant happening during the performances, but they had almost given up going to other types of theatrical entertainment because of hooliganism.

It is strange to think that the current phenomenon of violence in sport, which we almost take for granted, should have been a part of another type of entertainment some two hundred years ago, and I wonder if the present wave of unrest on the terraces of our sporting arenas will come to an end as abruptly as it did in the theatre. Tough measures were introduced during the very early part of Queen Victoria's reign, and thugs and hooligans were barred from attending theatrical performances. To encourage theatre managements to use tougher measures, the young Queen Victoria and her consort Albert made it known that they would be paying visits to the theatre. Private Command performances were given at nearly all the royal residences in Queen Victoria's reign; in fact, they were so numerous it is possible to mention only a few. The Queen invited Charles Kean (son of the great Edmund) to present a series of plays at Windsor Castle, and the whole of the Royal Family, including the children, watched the performances in the Rubens room. It was in her reign that the first theatre knight was created, Henry Irving, whose Becket was such an enormous success that the Queen ordered a Command Performance to be given at Windsor Castle. Many people believed that the Prince of Wales had persuaded his mother to honour this fine actor — a controversial action at the time.

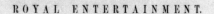

Programme of *The Rivals* printed on paper lace, 21 November 1855 and, *opposite,* Charles Kean's letter to Mr Wigan informing him of a change of date for *The Rivals* at Windsor Castle. Letter dated 3 November 1855. *By courtesy of Theatre Museum*

Dear Sir,

I beg to inform you that I have this moment rec'd a note from Col Phipps, informing me that the date is changed from the 22nd to the 21st for the performance of the Rivals at Windsor Castle — Yours faithfully Charles Kean.

Saturday
3 Nov 1855

One of the most curious Commands was to the Richardson family of Crosthwaite, near the town of Keswick in Cumberland, and it is worth recording the circumstances that brought this about. Mr Richardson, a mason by trade, worked with the rocks in the mountains, which taught him that many different sounds might be extracted from the raw materials he met with in the course of his labours. Being convinced that the fragments of the rocks might be collected and arranged to form musical instruments gave him the idea of forming a 'rock band'. He commenced work in 1827, first collecting the stones from the mighty Skiddaw mountain which he knew would be best suited for his purpose. Richardson bore these stones from the mountain to his home, a considerable distance, which was an immense labour. So, too, was the shaping of the stones, chiselling and hammering the rough pieces to the right state of the various instruments he had in mind. The softest tones of the 'Lascivious Lute', the shrill sounds of the fife, the bell-like quality of the piano, the sonorous peals of the organ were all to be heard from the stones of Skiddaw. In all, his work took thirteen years of labour and perseverance under circumstances few would understand. Richardson finally had a collection of stones giving him thirty-four different notes, plus a second collection of twenty-five semi-tones. To complete the Rock, Bell and Steel Band, which had been his original ambition, he added a similar number of tuned steel bars and forty-two brass bells. His enormous labours were rewarded a few years later, when with his family he was commanded to Buckingham Palace to give a performance for the Royal Family. Queen Victoria was so impressed that she commanded two further performances of the 'Rock, Bell and Steel Band', and quite naturally the publicity from all this opened the doors to further performances in London. This was just reward for the painstaking years that Mr Richardson had been through. Perhaps we could say that Queen Victoria made popular the first 'rock' music one hundred and thirty years ago.

Prince Albert's interest in the theatre lacked the enthusiasm of his Queen but he was always prepared to arrange theatrical occasions which

Richardson's Rock, Bell and Steel Band commanded to Buckingham Palace by Queen Victoria in the mid-1840s. The instrument is now in the Fitz Park Museum at Keswick in Cumbria. *Photograph courtesy of Fitz Park Museum*

State visit of Queen Victoria, Prince Albert, the Emperor Napoleon and his Empress at the Royal Italian Opera, 19 April 1855. *Harry R. Beard Collection, by courtesy of Theatre Museum*

he knew would please her. When Albert's cousin Victoire visited this country with her new husband the Duke of Nemors in 1841, Albert arranged for Charles Kemble and his company to perform a series of light plays at Windsor Castle. He also commanded a performance by the Astley Tumblers whom Albert had first seen in Coburg. This was a surprise for Victoire's birthday during the visit, and sent the royal ladies into ecstasies. The Queen later told Victoire that she had never enjoyed herself so much before. A performance of a whole pantomime produced by Edmund Yates was presented in 1855 at the Olympic Theatre by Royal Command of the Queen, with the Prince Consort and the fourteen-year-old Prince of Wales in the audience.

There were nearly always plays commanded to Windsor for Christmas, and opera was also occasionally performed at the Castle, the cast and orchestra being brought down to Windsor by special train. On one occasion Francisco Tamagno arrived too late to try out his voice in the Waterloo Gallery, where the accoustics were not very good. Francisco at one point during the performance let himself go with such force that the Queen, who was as usual sitting in the front row, almost had her cap blown off.

After Prince Albert's death the Queen declined to attend any entertainments in London, and it took a long time for the gloom to lift before she would even command performances of any description at

Court. One of the first was a performance of *The Gondoliers* in 1891. She had a great liking for Gilbert and Sullivan, and her knowledge of the operas was remarkable. When she was an old lady she sang a duet from *Patience* with Mr Alick Yorke. Obeying the Royal Command, Mr Yorke began, 'Prithee pretty maiden, will you marry me?' When Victoria's turn came, a very clear soft voice sang, 'Gentle sir, although to marry I'm inclined. . .' In the middle of the song the little Queen stopped to say, 'You know, Mr Yorke, I was taught singing by Mendelssohn.'

One afternoon on the terrace at Windsor Castle Queen Victoria was attracted by an air being played by the Guards Band. It was in fact a low comedy song called 'Come where the Booze is Cheaper', written by Sir George Dance, a most successful and ingenious musical comedy producer. The Queen sent a lady-in-waiting to ask the bandmaster what the tune might be. She was told it was a common music-hall song about strong drink and that the words ran: 'Come where the booze is cheaper, come where the pots hold more, Come where the boss is the deuce of a Joss, come to the pub next door.' This could have caused the remark 'We are not amused,' but in fact Queen Victoria accepted the fact that the popular music hall was a bawdy place, and could little have imagined that within twenty years a slightly more sophisticated version would be accepted as a legitimate entertainment through the goodwill of her son, and later her grandson.

The Prince of Wales, who had inherited his mother's enthusiasm and enjoyment of the theatre from an early age, must have been rather glad when the Queen once again interested herself in 'her actors' ' activities, as he had now become involved with some of the ladies of the theatrical profession and could enjoy himself to a greater extent without incurring his mother's displeasure. It is worth pointing out that Edward's genuine love for the theatre has sometimes been clouded by his reputation as a ladies' man. For instance, in 1865, as a member of the London Fire Service, he was first to a fire engine when he heard that the El Dorado Theatre in Leicester Square was ablaze, and tried his best to save the building. Incidentally, the site of the burned-out El Dorado was used to build the Empire Theatre of Varieties.

Edward loved the big theatrical occasion, and one in 1869 was as big as any. He took his Princess and the Crown Prince of Denmark to the Gaiety Theatre for a gala evening. The theatre was decorated with the Princess of Wales' favourite flower, the pink malmaison, and the atmosphere was heady with its clove scent.

The Prince was genuinely happy in the company of actors, and was often pleased to give them his time socially. Several years before his mother knighted Henry Irving, the prince gave a dinner at Marlborough

House in honour of some of the popular actors of the time, among them Charles Wyndham, Lionel Brough, Squire Bancroft, Arthur Cecil, Henry Irving and George Grossmith Senior. He repeated the event two or three years later and on that occasion was invited to dine with the actors at the Garrick Club, where they presented him with a gold cigar and cigarette case with the Prince of Wales crest mounted in diamonds. Later, as King, he was sometimes accompanied by actors on holiday.

The whole of the London theatre-going public was conscious of a more relaxed mood as Edward became more involved with the entertainment scene. Lily Langtry had been accepted as more than just a friend of the Prince of Wales, and had in fact been entertained by Princess Alexandra at Marlborough House. People were openly hearing stories about the theatrical ladies of the day:

> Mrs Pat Campbell, having had her share of dressing-room and drawing-room adventures, was heard to observe with relief when she married again — 'Ah, the deep, deep, bliss of the double bed, after the hurly-burly of the chaise longue.'[3]

Sarah Bernhardt was becoming a favourite of the Prince, and he was always ready to make an appearance at one of her performances to ensure it was a success. A music-hall singer called Miss Soldene owed a great deal to Edward's interest in her. Visiting a farming show in London, he was shown a portrait of the lady, a very pretty girl, and was told she was appearing at a music hall in Islington. The Prince arranged to visit the venue, which not unnaturally caused quite a stir. Miss Soldene's name was made overnight, and she went on to become a star of operetta. When the Can-Can was introduced to the Lyceum and Alhambra, Edward took Alexandra along to it and gave a seal of approval to the lighter London theatre.

Even abroad the Prince of Wales interested himself in the unusual in the entertainment world. On a visit to Canada he went to watch Blondin, the French acrobat, cross Niagara Falls on a tightrope. Blondin made several crossings of the Falls, standing on his head, turning somersaults and carrying a man on his back. Edward met the acrobat and congratulated him on these daring feats, and when Blondin offered to carry him over the Falls, Edward accepted — but was later advised not to undertake such a dangerous mission. Instead Blondin decided to cross the Falls on stilts in honour of the royal guest. In recognition of this the Prince sent him sixty sovereigns.

Even the beach pierrots were not forgotten. A concert party, led by banjoist Clifford Essex, was commanded to appear on the lawns of the Royal Yacht Squadron at Cowes in the Isle of Wight, during a visit by the Prince's nephew, Kaiser Wilhelm. This command came about because one of the troupe had taught the Prince of Wales to play the banjo.

The crowning of Edward VII heralded a new gay and light-hearted mood which was to sweep the country after the rather austere years of his mother's widowhood, and this mood was reflected in the theatre. Edward had been advised on his theatrical activities since the early 1870s by George Ashton, who ran a ticket agency in Bond Street. Ashton was a young man when he first met the then Prince of Wales through his boss, a Mr Mitchell, who originally owned the ticket agency. Ashton became a powerful influence in the theatre in London until 1925. He worked as hard as he did in organising royal theatrical occasions more for the love of it than for the financial gain. He played a big part in organising the first Royal Command Variety Performance.

The King's friendship with the great George Edwards was well known, not only because of the monarch's interest in the theatre but also because of their mutual enthusiasm for horse racing. They would attend the principal meetings and compare form and turf conditions. The King was a lover of the race track, and his horses won the Derby three times and the Grand National once.

The King and Queen were in the Royal Box when George Edwards' production of *The Orchid* opened at the New Gaiety in October 1903, starring a new and bright star, Gertie Miller. Edwards knew that *The Orchid* would be a success, and once it was safely established he started work on the *Duchess of Dantzig*, which he had wanted to produce for some time. His enthusiasm for this proposed show was such that he went to Windsor Castle and, with the help of the King, checked the designs for the Napoleonic uniforms with the prints in the Windsor collection.

In 1904 Oswald Stoll's great dream of owning the finest theatre in London had materialised when the Coliseum opened its doors to the public. It had been designed with a lift to take the audience to the upper parts of the building. Another innovation was a single-track tramline laid from a private foyer, on which a glass coach ran to the entrance of the Royal Box, where it served as an ante-room for the 'Box'. A few weeks after the opening, Edward and Alexandra paid a visit to the Coliseum, but when they entered the coach it refused to start. The King suggested that they walk to the Royal Box and the coach was never used again, though the place where the lines were laid can still be traced in the floor.

In June 1907 *The Merry Widow* made its début at Daly's Theatre and set London alight with its gorgeous costumes and fine music. The Merry Widow 'hat' was being worn by everyone, and it was said that a million pounds had been taken at the box office. A certain amount of this success

Command performance of *A Man's Shadow* by Beerbohm Tree's company in the Waterloo Chamber, Windsor Castle, 17 November 1904. Front row, left to right: King Carlos of Portugal, Queen Alexandra, Queen Amélie, King Edward VII. The floral decorations surrounding the stage were magnificent. *Drawing from the Illustrated London News, by courtesy of Theatre Museum*

SANDRINGHAM

PROGRAMME

NOVEMBER 26TH, 1901

" S

CHARLES DICK

B (

Adapted for the

Performed by Mr. SEYM(
Vaudev

Ebenezer Scrooge -   -
The Ghost of Jacob Marley
Fred. Wayland (*Scrooge's Ne*
Bob Cratchitt (*Scrooge's Cler*
Mr. Middlemark -   -   -
Mr. Worthington   -   -
Mrs. Fred. Wayland -   -
Mrs. Cratchitt -   -   -
Tiny Tim
Peter -   -⎫
Martha   -   ⎪   *The Cratc*
Belinda   -   ⎬   *Childre*
A Small Boy ⎪
A Small Girl ⎭
The Boy Scrooge   -   -
Fanny (*his Sister*) -   -

Two Poor Waifs   -   -

Scrooge's Sweetheart   -

Children at Fred. Wayland's
    Christmas Party

Offices and Chambers of

· The Carols Sung b
The Incidental Music
Electrical Effect
Mechanis

ANCE GIVEN BEFORE

EDWARD VII.

AT SANDRINGHAM, BEING THE

PRINCESS CHARLES OF DENMARK

GE,"

HRISTMAS CAROL,

c Act,

C. BUCKSTONE.

S and the Company from the
, London.

s :

Mr. SEYMOUR HICKS
Mr. HOLBROOK BLINN
Mr. STANLEY BRETT
Mr. COMPTON COUTTS
Mr. J. C. BUCKSTONE
Mr. GEORGE MUDIE, Jun.
Miss HILDA ANTONY
Miss FLORENCE LLOYD
Master GEORGE HERSEE
Master REGINALD DENNY
Miss ANNIE BARKMAN
Miss KATIE MAY
Master ALFRED SAWYER
Miss P. CAMPBELL
Master EWART HOOPER
Miss DAISY THIMM
Miss DAISY LEE
Miss ETHEL LEE
Miss EDITH HESLEWOOD
Miss KELLY
Miss DAVIS
Master RANDALL
Master ROBERTSON

czer Scrooge. W. HARFORD

's Choir of Children.
by Miss DORA BRIGHT
THOMAS J. DIGBY.
H. TONKIN

MR. DAN LENO

From the London Pavilion and Drury Lane Theatre.

———

" PAPA'S WIFE,"

A Musical Duologue, in One Act,

By SEYMOUR HICKS *and* F. C. PHILLIPS

Music by ELLALINE TERRISS

———

CHARACTERS :

Kate Weatherby   -   -   -   -   Miss ELLALINE TERRISS

Gerald Singleton   -   -   -   -   Mr. SEYMOUR HICKS

William   -   (*a Servant*)   -   -   Mr. STANLEY BRETT

———

SCENE : *A Drawing-Room.   Nine o'clock at Night.*

———

Stage Manager   -   -   Mr. GEORGE FIELDER

Musical Director   -   -   Mr. WALTER SLAUGHTER

Business Manager -   -   Mr. HERBERT CLARK
(For Messrs. Gatti and Frohman.)

SUGGESTED

Y MR. GEORGE ASHTON, OF

ERSONALLY SUPERINTENDED

ERTAINMENT.

Previous page: Dan Leno was the first variety artiste to be commanded by a reigning monarch. Sandringham, 1901. *Above*: A fancy dress ball was held annually at the Theatre Royal Drury Lane until the early 1900s. Dan Leno won it on three occasions. Depicted here as Richard III. *By courtesy of Audrey Leno*

was surely due to the King's patronage of the musical comedy. He had visited Daly's four times during the run.

It was obvious that the monarch was enjoying the theatre which he had done so much to encourage. His tastes were varied, and his enthusiasm for what he saw was plain to see. The Empire Leicester Square, considered to be not quite respectable in the early 1900s, was patronised by King Edward and Queen Alexandra, and if this visit by their majesties surprised some people, it was all part of Edward's liking for the music hall. After all, he had already commanded some of the leading music-hall artistes at that time to Sandringham, including Bransby Williams, Dan Leno and Albert Chevalier.

Dan Leno had, in 1901, been the first variety artiste ever to be commanded by a reigning monarch. This giant among comedians, star of Drury Lane pantomime and world clog dancing champion, was also recognised as having great potential as a straight actor, a potential which would surely have been fulfilled had he lived long enough to be given the opportunity. He was earning £300 a week by 1900, a huge sum of money by any standards. After the command at Sandringham for Edward VII, the King presented him with a diamond tie-pin bearing a crown and His Majesty's initials. Dan Leno was now titled 'The Court Jester'. I must put the record straight about Leno's death. It has been stated by different sources that he went mad and died in a lunatic asylum. This is not true. He died of a serious illness in hospital at the age of 43, when his extraordinary talents were at their peak.

The King's comparatively short reign ended in 1910, but he had earned the grateful thanks of the theatrical fraternity, for he had been their fan and their friend. It was almost a personal loss to many artistes, and they wondered whether they would ever know another such monarch who appeared to have cared so much for them and their theatre. Edward VII had set a pattern which was, happily, to be continued by future monarchs.

Notes

1. W. Macqueen-Pope, *Haymarket — Theatre of Perfection* (W. H. Allen, 1948), p. 166.
2. W. Macqueen-Pope, *Theatre Royal Drury Lane* (W. H. Allen, 1945), p. 205.
3. Allen Andrews, *The Follies of King Edward VII* (Lexington Press, 1975).

2

CINDERELLA
GOES TO THE BALL

The stability of the country was under strain when George V came to the throne. Apart from the delicate balance of power held by Asquith — to keep it he had to make a deal with Balfour — the suffragette movement was gaining momentum and the Irish Nationalist MPs held the key to his position in the House of Commons. A daunting time for any monarch, but more so perhaps for George V, as he was inexperienced in state affairs, having spent so much of his early life in the Royal Navy. The King was a sensitive man, and was concerned about many of the changes that were taking place. Significant changes had of course taken place in the theatre by 1910, particularly the public's fast-growing interest in the variety theatre which had its roots in the taverns and music halls of the late nineteenth century. The words 'music hall' were exactly what they implied, a hall for the presentation of music — a place where solo turns performed to an audience who had basically gone to drink. Most of these halls were attached to public houses, perhaps the most famous being Wilton's near Tower Bridge. This area was frequented by seamen when London was a flourishing port. The near vicinity was populated by many prostitutes who earned their living from the sailors and the neighbourhood was also frequented by Jack the Ripper. On their majesties' accession, celebrations of the event included gala performances of opera, ballet and drama. The night at Covent Garden impressed everyone with its opulence; the cast included Nellie Melba, Tetrazzini and their companies, as well as the Diaghilev Ballet with Nijinsky. The King's guests included European and Eastern princes and princesses; in all, the royal party numbered over a hundred. It was a night for Covent Garden that could never be repeated. The performance was followed by a ball at Grosvenor House attended by their majesties. Hardly had they time to get their breath back when the next evening they attended what can only be described as an extravaganza of monumental proportions given by the legitimate theatre at His Majesty's in the Haymarket.

If the organisers were hoping that sheer quantity and length of performance would out-do the previous evening at 'The Garden', then they succeeded. The cast numbered five hundred, including Henry Ainley, Ellen Terry, George Arliss, Edmund Gwenn, Godfrey Tearle, Charles Wyndham, Marie Tempest, George Alexander, Lily Langtry, Charles Hawtrey, Mrs Patrick Campbell, Beerbohm Tree, who had been one of the organisers, and so on, and so on. There were excerpts from *The Merry Wives of Windsor, Julius Caesar, The Critic*, etc., etc.

George V was no intellectual, but being a dutiful man was quite prepared to continue the Royal Family's patronage of the arts. Queen Mary, on the other hand, was soon to show that she was an enthusiastic follower of the legitimate stage. It was clear that the King's taste was for the lighter side of the theatre, and in a roundabout way he cast one of the actors in a new Daly's theatre production, *The Count of Luxembourg*. His Majesty had met George Edwardes, who was producing the show, before he came to the throne, and subsequently mentioned an artiste, Bertram Wallis, whom he had admired. Edwardes went to see Wallis and engaged him for the *Count*. The music for this production was by Franz Lehar, who had written the music for *The Merry Widow*. The show was an immediate success, and so was Bertram Wallis, who quickly became the talk of the town and something of a matinée idol amongst the ladies.

George V had certainly proved to be a very discerning and successful talent scout for George Edwardes. The King and Queen were present at the first night, which was also another triumph for the magical Lily Elsie, though she was recovering from an operation and only managed to finish the performance with the help of pain-killing injections.

In 1910 Edward Moss, the boss of the Moss Empire theatre circuit, had quietly been putting out feelers in influential quarters to find out whether a Royal Gala occasion involving variety and music-hall artistes could be staged. With the help of George Ashton it was finally arranged and agreed by His Majesty that he should command a Royal Variety Performance during his Coronation year visit to Edinburgh. The venue was to be the Empire Palace Theatre there, the then head office of the Moss circuit. Can you imagine the elation and joy that the music hall must have felt in finally being recognised with its own 'Royal occasion'? But tragedy was to strike before the performance could take place. The theatre was burned down on 9 May 1911, and several lives lost. The royal performance was cancelled, and George V sent a letter of condolence to the relatives of those who died. The world-famous illusionist Lafayette, who was appearing at the theatre at the time with his company, perished in the fire, along with two of his assistants. The Iron, which separates the stage of a theatre from the auditorium, was lowered very quickly, thus containing the fire to the stage area where it

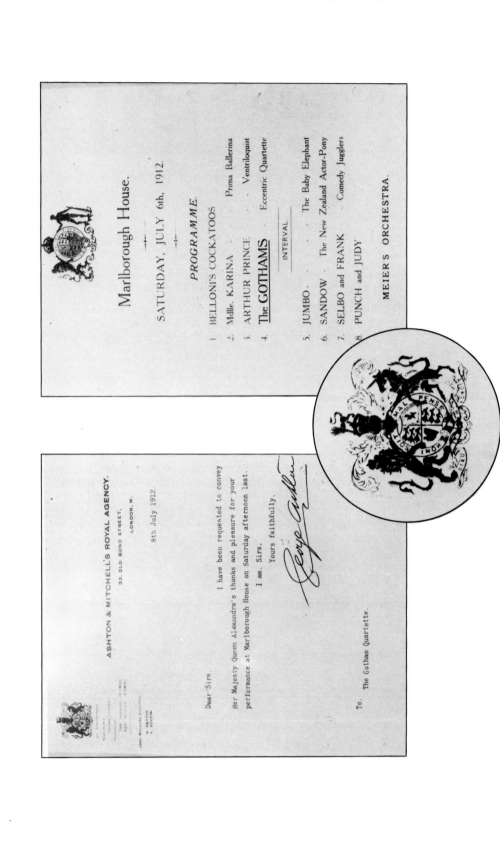

Marlborough House.

SATURDAY, JULY 6th, 1912.

PROGRAMME.

1. BELLONI'S COCKATOOS
2. Mdlle. KARINA - Prima Ballerina
3. ARTHUR PRINCE - Ventriloquist
4. The GOTHAMS - Eccentric Quartette

INTERVAL

5. JUMBO - The Baby Elephant
6. SANDOW - The New Zealand Actor-Pony
7. SELBO and FRANK - Comedy Jugglers
8. PUNCH and JUDY

MEIER'S ORCHESTRA.

ASHTON & MITCHELL'S ROYAL AGENCY.

33, OLD BOND STREET,

LONDON. W.

8th July 1912.

Dear Sirs,

I have been requested to convey
Her Majesty Queen Alexandra's thanks and pleasure for your
performance at Marlborough House on Saturday afternoon last.

I am, Sirs,

Yours faithfully,

George Arthur

To. The Gotham Quartette.

had started. Some members of the back-stage staff and two members of the orchestra died in the blaze. There were fifteen hundred people in the audience that night, and miraculously all got out of the theatre alive. A strange action on the part of the manager when the fire was in progress was to rush on to the front of the stage and shout to the band, 'Play God Save the King!' A footnote to this is that Lafayette, whose real name was Sigmund Neuburger and who came originally from Baden-Baden, had a dog he was passionately fond of. The day before the fire the dog died, so Lafayette had it embalmed and interred in a vault in Piers Hill cemetery near the Firth of Forth and made a will asking to be buried beside it. The remains of Lafayette's body were going to be cremated, but before this could be done a further body was found in the debris which was positively identified as that of Lafayette. The first body was that of his principal assistant, who was almost identical to him and used by the illusionist as a double for his various tricks. His ashes were subsequently put in the tomb with his embalmed dog, the urn with the ashes nestling between the dog's paws.

A Royal Command performance was staged at Drury Lane in 1911, but this was for the legitimate theatre. It was presented at the request of the King for his cousin Kaiser Wilhelm II who was on a visit to this country to unveil a memorial to his Grandmother, Queen Victoria. For some reason or other it was decided to do a revival of 'Money', and whether it was the play or the haste with which it was produced by a now slightly potty Squire Bancroft, or a culmination of all three, is not certain, but the result was a disaster. The cast list read like a 'Who's Who' of the Theatre, many of them taking walk-on parts for the evening. The Kaiser was seen during the evening patting his bad hand in an attempt to applaud actors who didn't know their lines. A member of the audience said, 'If all this doesn't precipitate a war with Germany, I'll eat my hat!'[1]

In July 1912 a Royal Command Variety Performance was eventually staged in London at the Palace Theatre. Most of the big variety and music-hall names of that time took part, with the exception of Marie Lloyd and Albert Chevalier. It was felt by the organisers that Marie Lloyd was a little too vulgar for a royal occasion, particularly as music hall had only just become respectable, and her act might mar its newly won status. This did seem a pity, as Marie Lloyd was then one of the most popular and much loved performers of the music hall. The omission

---

Opposite: programme of private command performance at Marlborough House, 6 July 1912, and letter of thanks to the 'Gothams' from the organiser George Ashton. *By courtesy of Grand Order of Water Rats*

1 Harry Blake	37 Marie Kendall	73 Edward E. Ford	107 Harry Webber
2 Arthur Revell	38 Fred Curran	74 Cliff Ryland	108 R.H. Douglass
3 Harry Stelling	39 Alfred Lester	75 Irene Rose	100 La Pia
4 Alice Tremayne	40 Novikoff	76 Fred Kitchen	109 Florrie Forde
5 Marguerite Broadfootte	41 Percy Delevine	77 Florence Smithers	111 Florrie Gallimore
6 Cinquevalli	42 Harriet Vernon	78 Arthur Leonard	112 Edith Evelyn
7 George D'Albert	43 David Devant	79 Ryder Slone	113 Tom Clare
8 Charles Colborn	44 Harry Delevine	80 'My Fancy'	114 Ella Shields
9 Harry Grattan	45 J.W. Rowley	81 Esta Stella	115 Harry Ford
10 Wilkie Bard	46 Martin Adeson	82 Gracie Whiteford	116 Flora Cromer
11 Vesta Tilley	47 Alexandra Dagmar	82A Tom Edward's	117 William Downes
12 Arthur Prince	48 Mrs Adeson	dummy	118 Charles Langford
13 John Le Hay	49 Harry Lauder	83 Fred Sinclair	119 J.W. Wilson
14 Babs	50 T.E. Dunville	84 Seth Egbert	120 Deane Tribune
15 Harry Claff	51 Kate Carney	85 J. Alexandre	121 Bob Leonard
16 Beatie	52 Harry Tate	86 Harry Freeman	122 Jennie Leonard
17 G.H. Chirgwin	53 Fred Emney	87 Albert Egbert	123 Cecilia Macarte
18 Billy Williams	54 George Bastow	88 W.F. Frame	124 George Newham
19 May Law	55 Joe Tennyson	89 G. Hughes	125 Fred Latimer
20 Pavlova	56 Charles Whittle	90 Dave Carter	126 Joe Boganny
21 Jack Marks	57 J.W. Tate	91 Elsie Finney	127 Sydney James
22 George Gray	58 Clarice Mayne	92 Billie Bint	128 Alfred Lotto
23 George Leyton	59 Peggy Pryde	93 Julia Macarte	129 Clara Lilo
24 Edwin Barwick	60 Tom Woottwell	94 Will Kellino	130 Ernest Otto
25 Herbert Darnley	61 Harry Champion	95 Jack Lorimer	131 Gus McNaughton
26 Cecilia Loftus	62 Minnie Duncan	96 Harry Weldon	132 Fred McNaughton
27 Vasco	63 Arthur Godfrey	97 George French	133 Horace Wheatley
28 Fanny Fields	64 George Robey	98 Emilie D'Alton	134 Arthur Rigby
29 Cruickshank	65 Gus Elen	99 Ella Retford	135 Albert Atlas
30 Diana Hope	66 Barclay Gammon	100 Edmund Edmunds	136 Carlton
31 Fred Farren	67 Albert Le Fre	101 Albert Edmunds	137 Marriott Edgar
32 Ida Crispi	68 Arthur Gallimore	102 'Papa' Brown	138 Lizzie Collins
33 James Stewart	69 James Finney	103 Tom Stuart	139 F.V. St Clair
34 Pipifax	70 Lupino Lane	104 Harry Randall	140 Ada Cerito
35 Panlo	71 Charles McConnell	105 Marie Loftus	141 Fred Herbert
36 Charles Austin	72 Joe McConnell	106 W.J. Churchill	142 Walter Munro

Variety's garden party: the finale of the first Royal Command Variety Performance at London's Palace Theatre, 1 July 1912. *By courtesy of The Raymond Mander & Joe Mitchenson Theatre Collection* of Albert Chevalier was just as strange, remembering he had already been privately commanded to Sandringham by Edward VII.

Apart from the King and Queen at the Palace on that evening there were, among others, the King's sister Princess Victoria, his cousin Princess Victoria of Schleswig-Holstein, her mother Princess Christian, Queen Mary's brother and his wife the Duke and Duchess of Teck, the King's aunt Princess Henry of Battenberg and his uncle Prince Arthur of Connaught. The ever helpful George Ashton was amongst the welcoming party at the theatre. The front of the Royal Box had been extended for the occasion, making it easy for their majesties to see the entire stage area, and this arrangement in turn allowed the whole audience to see the Royal Family.

> To what a beautiful and lordly pleasure house the King and Queen came! The house in Shaftesbury Avenue has been always looked upon as one of the most magnificent in Europe, but the fine architectural features of the building, decorated as they were with thousands of roses, bore an aspect of great charm. The coup d'oeil from the centre of the stalls to the roof was of a floral fairyland — a fit habitat indeed for Terpsichore, Euterpe, and Thalia. At the rear and sides of the stalls prettily designed panelling had been placed in position, giving through decorative trellis work — largely employed — a superb floral vista effect, the visitor having the impression of being seated in a lovely Italian garden. Rambler roses, mostly crimson and pink, climbed up on each side of the front of the stage, culminating at the top of the proscenium arch in a large wreath, from which depended garlands of great beauty, transforming the theatre into a perfect bower of roses. The roof glinted with some three hundred tiny bulbs peeping out from yellow roses. The Royal box, which was on the O.P. [opposite prompter] side was festooned with a mass of pink ramblers, and a similar scheme of decoration was carried out in the two boxes opposite. A landing on the staircase to the dress circle was a combination of tall branches of variegated maple, with pink hydrangeas, coleus and lilies. The new act drop is in imitation of Beauvalis tapestry, the central painting being a representation of Fontain's picture of the gardens at Versailles, the original of which is at the South Kensington Museum. For richness of colour, for tastefulness of arrangement, and for real prettiness the general effect would be difficult to excel, and it is wonderfully chaste and artistic.[2]

The overture 'Britannia' played by the Palace orchestra, who were to cover themselves with glory on the night, heralded the start of the greatest music-hall bill ever gathered together under one roof. It included G. H. Chirgwin 'The White Eyed Kaffir', Vesta Tilley the male impersonator, Little Tich, Fanny Fields, Harry Tate, Clarice Mayne and 'That' (J. W. Tate), George Robey 'The Prime Minister of Mirth', Arthur Pince and 'Jim', Alfred Lester, Wilkie Bard, Anna Pavlova with members of the Russian ballet, and Harry Lauder. In the magnificent finale, 'Variety's Garden Party', nearly one hundred and fifty other well known artistes of the day brought this first Royal Command Variety Performance to a close. Harry Tate's motoring sketch brought peals of laughter from the King and the royal party. Alfred Lester's Village Fire Brigade was received with great enthusiasm. Clarice Mayne, returning to the Palace where she was so popular, was a big success, and so too was George Robey, with his amazing delivery, fruity voice and cheeky looks to the audience. Harry Lauder, who was a favourite of King George, sang his own composition, 'Roamin' in the Gloamin' '.

Harry Tate saved this Royal Command Performance from an embarrassing situation. One of the preceding acts to Tate's was Vesta Tilley, the male impersonator, and it was noted that from that time on Queen Mary held her programme in front of her face. The Queen apparently thought it quite wrong that a woman should dress up as a man and wear trousers. The audience was aware of Her Majesty's obvious displeasure, which had a dampening effect on their reaction to the show. Within a few minutes of Harry Tate starting his motoring sketch, however, George V was seen to be laughing; Queen Mary

Scroll presented to Harry Freeman commemorating his appearance in the Royal Command Variety Performance, 1 July 1912. *By courtesy of Grand Order of Water Rats*

lowered her programme and she too began to laugh — which meant that the rest of the audience could relax and enjoy the buffoonery of Tate. Harry's son Ronnie was a spectator at the show, and at the end Harry told Ronnie to go up to the Royal Box and see if there might be a souvenir programme left there. There was, the velvet-covered one which had been presented to Queen Mary. It is now in Ronnie's safe keeping and is a treasured possession.

> King George looked upon his night at the Palace in the light of a lover of true Bohemianism, and his attitude towards the show was a sheer delight to watch. The Royal party stayed to the end, and His Majesty bowed from the Royal Box in acknowledgement of the ringing cheers which rose from every part of the house at the conclusion of the National anthem.[3]

The proceeds of this charity performance were donated to the Variety Artistes Benevolent Fund at the request of George V, to help maintain Brinsworth House, a nursing home for retired variety performers which had been opened in 1911.

The possibility of another Royal Variety Performance was discussed by various theatrical managements the following year, but it was thought an inopportune time to approach His Majesty, as he had other far-reaching problems. Even while the situation in Ireland was being debated, the King's attention, and that of the whole country, was switched to a little-known area in Europe known as Serbia. By the early summer of 1914 it looked as if most of the countries of Europe were merely squabbling amongst themselves. Little did anyone think that within a few short weeks they, and Britain with them, would be plunged into the bloodiest war in history. The King went almost immediately to France, visiting regiments of the British Expeditionary force who had been committed to go to the aid of Belgium and France. His Majesty was determined to give them encouragement in the early days of the conflict. He visited the French battlefields five times in all during the war.

The theatre at home, once over the initial shock of hostilities, got down to the business of keeping up the morale of the public and service-men on leave in London. *Tonight's The Night*, starring George Grossmith, opened at the Gaiety Theatre early in 1915. The big number in the show featured by Grossmith was 'They Didn't Believe Me' which was to be sung, whistled and hummed by millions of people for a very long time. *Tonight's The Night* made Leslie Henson a star who was to shine for many years in practically every theatre in the West End at some time or another. Servicemen would cluster around the stage door of the Gaiety during their few brief days' leave from France. The possibility of supper with a Gaiety Girl was something worth waiting for.

One night the war came close to the Gaiety. A bomb fell outside the Lyceum Theatre just across the way, immediately followed by another which struck 'The Bell' public house on the corner of Exeter and Wellington Streets. One of the Gaiety electricians was killed, also a messenger boy. A third bomb fell in the road between the Gaiety and the Strand theatres. The Gaiety call boy, Jimmy Wickham, who was out on an errand, was severely injured and was taken to Charing Cross Hospital with a large piece of bomb embedded over his heart. King George heard about the case, and visited him in hospital.[4]

Both the King and Queen Mary did all they could to cheer and encourage all the worthy causes that the war effort needed. Early on they attended a charity matinée at the Palladium in aid of the Chelsea Hospital for Women. An amusing anecdote concerning King George during the First World War was an occasion when he gave a party for some wounded soldiers at Buckingham Palace.

Herman Finck from the Palace Theatre was there with his orchestra to play for them. Finck was told that if the King came into the room during the Concert he was not to interrupt the programme, as it was an entirely informal occasion. One of the items was a collection of popular songs under the title of 'Melodious Memories', and it was during this that the King came in, just as the orchestra had started playing 'Hush, Hush, Here Comes The Bogey Man'. It was the King who led the laughter in which the soldier audience delightedly joined.[5]

One of His Majesty's favourite entertainers, George Robey, was not only keeping theatre audiences entertained with his appearances in various shows but was also a tireless worker for charity, collecting thousands of pounds for various causes. France decorated him with the Legion of Honour in recognition of his raising £14,000 for the French Red Cross. He was also a special constable and a member of the Volunteer Motor Transport Corps, ferrying soldiers from one main line station in London to another, either when they were going on leave or returning to France for another spell in the trenches. His almost fanatical desire to keep fit (he was on the wrong side of forty) certainly gave him the energy to do all this, plus of course his nightly performances at the theatre. He starred in the *Bing Boys*, where his duet with Vi Loraine — 'If You Were the Only Girl in the World' — was delighting audiences nightly. A young man called Ivor Novello made his début as a composer at about this time, when he co-wrote the score with Jerome Kern for the new Gaiety production that followed — *Tonight's the Night*. Novello, of course, wrote one of the most sensitive and nostalgic war songs ever — 'Keep the Home Fires Burning', still thought of today along with 'Pack Up your Troubles' and 'It's a Long Way to Tipperary' when people talk of the Great War. In later years Ivor Novello was to become a great showman, particularly at Drury Lane.

King George paid a visit to Drury Lane for a matinée during the war, and took the opportunity to knight Frank Benson, the Shakespearian actor-manager — the only occasion I know of an actor being knighted 'on the premises'.

A propaganda film was made in 1917 by the cinema king D. W. Griffith. The film was silent of course, and contained gruesome scenes of the fighting in France. George V, who had a copy of the film shown to him at Windsor, wrote a review for the *Daily Mail* which was used for advance publicity wherever the film was shown. It was also shown to a select audience from both Houses of Parliament. One Lord asked to be put as near as possible, as he was hard of hearing. Afterwards he complained that somehow or other the film had turned him completely deaf, and that he would never go and see another one of these new-fangled picture shows again. It appears no one told him that the film was silent.

Before the war had finished an entertainment revolution was taking place in America that was very soon to be felt in Britain. Dixieland jazz was turning audiences who experienced it into liberated beings, as the foot-tapping and hip-wiggling quickly gained a following. Mind you, this entertainment certainly had its critics. The Seven Spades Jazz Band came to this country in 1917, but it was the Original Dixieland Jazz Band, or O.D.J.B. as they were called, who really made their mark over here. They were booked for a season at the London Pavilion sharing the bill with 'The Prime Minister of Mirth', George Robey. Robey hated their music and told the manager, 'Either they go, or I do.' They went. The music did have an air of sensuousness, a racy rhythm and some of the atmosphere of the brothels of New Orleans from whence it originated. Up to that time music had been melodically simple, but ragtime was here to stay.

During the Great War many artistes and managements gave their time to entertain the troops and raise funds for various war charities. In recognition of all this George V conferred knighthoods on Oswald Stoll, Walter de Frece, Alfred Butt and Harry Lauder.

The King also commanded a Royal Performance in July 1919 at the London Coliseum which was to be organised by Oswald Stoll, who had remarked after the 1912 Variety Command Performance, 'Cinderella has gone to the ball.' The 1919 performance was in recognition of the charitable work of many variety artistes during the war. A patriotic finale, 'Pageant of Peace', with Sir Edward Elgar conducting the orchestra, brought this Command to its conclusion. Several artistes from the Royal Command Performance of 1912 took part, including George Robey and Vi Loraine, Arthur Prince and 'Jim', Clarice Mayne and 'That', Grock and partner, and the exalted Harry Tate, who was by now at the peak of his career.

Tate was again a great success with another motoring sketch. He had by now become a giant not only of the music hall but also revue. He starred at the London Hippodrome in show after show during the war, first in *Hello Tango*, then *Business as Usual, Razzle Dazzle* and *Box of Tricks*. Tate had begun his career as an impressionist, for which he had an uncanny gift. It wasn't only his voice: facially his impressions were superb. His George Robey impersonation was so good that when he and George were playing on the same bill for a week at the Manchester Palace, Robey did the first part of his act and Tate the second, and nobody knew the difference. Eventually he abandoned his impressions and developed the first of his unforgettable sketches. His 'motoring' was an immediate success, possibly because in real life he was a first-class mechanic and driver, so that he could get an enormous amount of comedy out of every aspect of motoring. He made a car, at that time a novelty, into a fun toy. Any strange mechanical device was called a 'Harry Tate contraption'. A small sample of the organised lunacy of Harry Tate that had made King George laugh at the 1912 Royal Command and again in 1919:

Scene: A typical London street with battered car outside Tate's house. Tate is in car along with son and chauffeur.

Friend: Where are you off to?
(Off)

Tate: I'm just going down to Portsmouth, taking my son back to the Naval College.

Friend: That's funny. I'm going down there too.
(Off)

Tate: Well, why not join us?

Friend: I can't very well, I've got the wife and family with me.
(Off)

Tate: Well, bring the wife too, there's plenty of room alongside my son, we can put the family in the tool box.

Friend: No, no, don't trouble, old man, I'll meet you down there . . .
(Off)

Tate: Goodbye — I'll be down there long before you. I'll order lunch. What will you have, Grouse or bread and dripping?

A perfectly reasonable conversation in a normal situation, until the ridiculous 'What will you have, Grouse or bread and dripping?' Harry Tate was a comedy actor, one of a handful of music-hall comedians who

Friends on stage and off — George Robey, left, and Harry Tate after a round of golf in the 1920s. Under Robey's signature he has added the opening line of his stage performances, 'Last Wednesday I think it was'. *Photograph courtesy of Ronnie Tate*

could have been a success in this age of television. He was considered by his fellow performers to be a comic genius, who could enslave an audience with a twitch of his trade mark, a red false moustache. Harry's son Ronnie, who appeared with his father in many of his sketches spanning twenty years or more, told me of his father's great sense of the ridiculous, for instance in his 'Office' sketch, where he would walk in and say to the office secretary:

> 'Good morning, any letters this morning? What, no letters, then we'd better write some. You know, we must get a bottom in this desk drawer, it's absurd, everything you put in the drawer goes into the waste paper basket. If you want to refer to anything, you have to go and see the dustman.'

He was generous in giving the laughs to his stooges, but of course it was a clever move because it allowed him to weave in and out of one absurdity to another.

A true story about Harry Tate was re-told by his close friend, Robb Wilton. Tate was appearing in a charity show in London when he was unexpectedly called to be presented to Queen Alexandra. He noticed, with some panic, that everybody took off their hats and bowed. Well, Harry didn't have a hat to take off, so he took off his moustache, bowed, and put it back on again. Nobody laughed more than the Queen.

Harry Tate was not only revered by his fellow professionals in the theatre, but was also a man of honour. Towards the end of 1920 Tate was invited to tour Canada with a revue that Albert de Corville was producing. De Corville, once secretary to Sir Thomas Lipton the tea merchant, had been producing many of the revues that Tate starred in during the war at the London Hippodrome. His son Ronnie was in the show, and told me that the tour of Canada was a great success but at the end of it De Corville disappeared, leaving the large cast stranded without money and without their fares home. Tate decided to take charge and quickly arranged to go over the border into America and try their luck there. They went all over California, in small towns and large, and ended up in Los Angeles. Even though the show had done good business wherever it went, it didn't really make any money because the cast was so large. However, in Los Angeles the company had a visit from Charlie Chaplin, who had worked with one of the cast when he was in Casey's Court in England. Chaplin bought out the theatre for a whole fortnight, and not only invited all his friends to 'come and see the great English revue with the very funny Harry Tate', but also invited the cast to meet many of the Hollywood film stars Chaplin knew. He also invited some of the principals of the show to have dinner at his home. The company went back through California to Canada to make their way back to

England. Tate had the money to get home, and the British Consul in Vancouver advised him to go and leave the chorus to earn the money for their fare by taking jobs as waitresses or even less respectable trades. Tate was very much against this, saying the girls came from good homes in England and he was going to make sure they got back safely. Harry paid all the fares of the chorus and a Canadian Pacific liner brought them home.

In the first ten years of his reign, George V had shown the music hall that the comic absurdity of its performers and their inconsequential buffoonery had given him a lot of pleasure. It might be a little bawdy, occasionally cheeky, but never, never blue; it was honest humour, and King George was a very honest man. The ensuing years were to cement even further the relationship between the sailor King and the changing styles in entertainment. The twenties would see the coming of regular wireless transmission, talking pictures, the establishment of night club entertainment in and around London, and because of the Royal Family's enthusiasm for the theatre, an annual Royal Variety Performance.

Notes

1. From an article by John East.
2. Extract from *British Music Hall*, by Raymond Mander and Joe Mitchenson (Gentry Book Publishers, 1965).
3. Ibid.
4. W. Macqueen-Pope, *Gaiety, Theatre of Enchantment* (W. H. Allen, 1949).
5. Ian Bevan, *Royal Performance* (Hutchinson, 1954).

3

'YOU AIN'T HEARD NOTHIN' YET'

Lloyd George had said that post-war Britain would be a land fit for heroes. George V certainly had to be a hero to deal with all the political ups and downs that were to emerge in the 1920s. His tact and conscientious understanding would certainly be put to good use, perhaps at times to the exclusion of his family, which must have grieved him, as he was a family man. His eldest son, the Prince of Wales, was becoming a popular figure with the man in the street, although the King thought him rather flippant in some of his actions, and expressed these thoughts in a letter to Edward's brother, the Duke of York. King George was an honest thinking man, and when Ramsay MacDonald formed a Labour government he wrote to his mother, Queen Alexandra, saying how intelligent he thought the Labour Ministers were, and that he hoped they would be given a fair chance to govern, even though they had different ideas from him, as they were socialists.

The social revolution in the twenties was dramatic, and for some difficult to understand. It was a revolution that the King had to understand as much as his subjects. The motor car was beginning to make its presence felt on the roads, and aeroplanes were becoming more than a novelty. Nearly everyone now smoked cigarettes. Fashions in ladies' clothes were changing with the shift and cloche hat, bringing a new word into the vocabulary — 'the flapper'. There was a tremendous determination among the female population to win the vote; indeed fundamental social change was taking place and people's expectations were rising after promises of a 'land fit for heroes'. But Britain was not quite the Utopia it proclaimed. Entertainment in the twenties would be conquering new horizons — already silent movies from America were flooding every hall capable of showing them. Charlie Chaplin, the Keystone Cops and the big silent extravaganzas were seriously challenging the music hall in this country.

One of the silent film impresarios at that time was Vivian Van Damm. He was probably one of the first movie entrepreneurs in this country. He was later to become world famous as proprietor of London's Windmill Theatre, and was responsible not only for the highly successful girlie revues but also for giving a first chance to many, many comedians and entertainers who eventually became stars. He presented the first great silent classic movies in this country, *The Four Horsemen of the Apocalypse* and *The Prisoner of Zenda*. Queen Mary and her two sons, the Prince of Wales and the Duke of Gloucester, went to see *The Four Horsemen* during its run in London. The Prince of Wales also went to see *The Prisoner of Zenda*, and as a result of these visits to the cinema Van Damm was asked by King George to show a full-length film in the royal apartments at Windsor Castle. It was probably the first time such an event had taken place there, and shows how the King was prepared to involve himself in the entertainment industry in general.

An ex-music-hall comedian, Harry Marlow, had been enlisted by the Variety Artistes Benevolent Fund (now known as the Entertainment Artistes Benevolent Fund) to raise money for those performers who were sick or had fallen on hard times, and to maintain Brinsworth House at

The first royal visit to a cinema, Marble Arch Pavilion, November 1924, to see the naval film *Zeebrugge*. Left to right: Earl Beatty, George V and Queen Mary. *Photograph courtesy of BBC Hulton Picture Library*

Twickenham — a house that was to become a haven for aged pros once their playing days were over. Harry Marlow had to find a way of making regular sums of money, mainly for Brinsworth. Remembering George V's enthusiasm and appreciation of the Royal Command performances of 1912 and 1919, Marlow wondered if it might be possible to organise an annual event of this kind. After various enquiries in royal circles as to this possibility and receiving favourable reaction, Marlow asked the King whether he would give his patronage to it. The King at once agreed, and so in 1921 a Royal Variety Performance was staged on 25 November at the London Hippodrome. This performance was the forerunner of many more. The days and weeks before the event were a worrying time for Marlow, as he had to convince not only members of his own profession but also the public, who he hoped would pay to see the royal show, that it would be the success he hoped for. The price for the better seats was three guineas and they weren't selling very well, but a few days before curtain-up a royal engagement was announced, that of the King's daughter, Princess Mary, to Viscount Lascelles, and the first public appearance of the engaged couple was to be at the Royal Variety Performance with King George and Queen Mary. This announcement guaranteed a full house for Harry Marlow and the Variety Artistes Benevolent Fund, which benefited handsomely.

George V was so delighted with the prospect of the royal show becoming an annual fund-raiser that he became a life patron of the VABF. This patronage was to be carried on by his son, George VI, Queen Elizabeth the Queen Mother and our present Queen. A slightly more varied cast was assembled for the 1922 royal performance in December of that year, again at the London Hippodrome, with the ventriloquist Arthur Prince and 'Jim' making their third royal appearance before His Majesty. Harry Weldon singing his by now famous Cockney songs was also included. The Scots actor/comedian Will Fyfe was a big hit, and it was probably this appearance that began his popularity south of the border.

By 1923 the division in society as far as entertainment was concerned was very noticeable. Well known London hotels were recruiting top musicians and cabaret artistes, many of them from across the Atlantic, to take advantage of the enthusiasm of the 'London Set' for the wave of swing and jazz that had already established itself in America. At a later date the hotel entertainment would become an enormous attraction with 'society' and a playground for a future King. For the music hall it was a time of competition, but the bosses of the large variety houses were not letting the grass grow under their feet. Theatres were now including a much greater variety of items in their productions. Circus performers, actors playing short scenes from well known plays and ballet companies were being integrated with the established music-hall artistes. All this was evident in the royal show of December 1923 at the London Coliseum. The performance included a one-act play starring Lewis Gilbert and Anne Trevor, the Lois Fuller Ballet, the Royal Albert Hall Orchestra, conducted by Sir Landon Ronald, and a popular music-hall sketch, 'The Disorderly Room' with its creator Tommy Handley, and Ralph Lynn and Tom Walls, who were already making a reputation for themselves in theatre farce. Tommy Handley had been a seaside concert party entertainer who graduated to the music halls, in which sphere he was never at his best, but his hey-day was to come later through the medium of radio.

The King and Queen always acknowledged how much they enjoyed being entertained at the theatre, either officially or on private visits. One of the Royal Family's favourite entertainers was Sir Harry Lauder. On one occasion King George and Queen Mary went to see Lauder at the Palace Theatre in London. George Ashton, who arranged all the royal visits to the theatre, told the Scots entertainer that their majesties would like to see him in the Box after the show. He naturally obeyed the command, and amongst other things the King asked him about his American trips and what songs he sang there. After a few minutes

Harry Lauder in the revue *Three Cheers* at the original Shaftesbury Theatre, 1916. On the bridge is James Macleod who later took over from Lauder when the revue went on tour. *Photograph courtesy of Marion Macleod*

Lauder left the box and went out into the corridor, where he bumped into George Ashton, who was talking to the Duke of Connaught, who had also attended the performance. He was introduced to the Duke, and after pleasantries on both sides Ashton moved away down the corridor. As he did so, Lauder said, 'Goodnight, George, and good luck.' At that moment King George came out of the Box and, looking in Lauder's direction, said, 'And goodnight and good luck to you, Harry.' As Lauder said in his autobiography, 'I was overwhelmed with confusion at the awful thought that I might be held as taking jocular liberties with the King, and stood riveted to the spot. But King George went off laughing heartily at his own joke.'

As far back as 1909 Harry Lauder had been commanded by royalty. It was on that occasion to Rufford Abbey, by Lord and Lady Saville who were entertaining King Edward VII. The Savilles had asked the King if he would like to have some entertainment during his stay, and the King said, 'Yes, tell Harry Lauder to come and sing to us.' Lauder went to Rufford Abbey with his son John, who was going to accompany him at the piano. He submitted his programme of songs to Lady Saville, who passed it on to the King. Lauder waited to know which songs His Majesty would like to hear. A message came back, 'Keep singing, the King will stop you when he's had enough.' The concert was held in one of the vaults of the Abbey, and the audience included some fifty or more guests of the Savilles, staying there for the Doncaster races. King Edward sat in between Lord and Lady Saville, surrounded by several members of the aristocracy, and behind them members of the Abbey staff. There was a small stage to perform on, and eventually Lauder was given the signal to begin by Lady Saville. After half a dozen songs, including 'I Love a Lassie', 'Tobermory', and 'Stop Your Ticklin' Jock', he still hadn't had a signal from the King to stop. After singing ten songs, all he had in his programme, Lauder stepped forward and announced that that was all he could sing because he had no more music with him. Exhausted, he went to the dressing-room to take a bath and relax for a while. Shortly after he had finished his concert the King's equerry came to tell him that His Majesty wanted to see him. Lauder said, 'What, like this, naked?' The official laughed, and said he would tell the King. King Edward waited until Lauder was ready, and when they did meet told the Scots entertainer how much he had enjoyed his performance. There can't be many people who have kept their monarch waiting while they had a bath, but then Harry Lauder was never overawed by kings, presidents or heads of state. Lauder, of course, was the first music-hall artiste to receive a knighthood. Perhaps it is fair to say that he wasn't just a music-hall 'turn', as it were. He must have been the first performer to present a one-man show, 'An Evening with Harry Lauder'. Apart from his fund-raising for war charities in this country, and his visits to the troops in France, he made coast-to-coast tours of America and Canada, where he raised thousands of pounds by simple theatre collections. It was at this time that his son John was killed on the field of battle in France.

One of the most sensational revolutions in entertainment in the twenties was the advent of broadcasting. The first regular Marconi wireless transmission took place on 14 February 1922 from a hut at Writtle, a village near Chelmsford in Essex — a daily programme of fifteen minutes. I wonder if Marconi, with even his technical knowledge and obvious foresight, would have imagined just what an effect wireless communication was going to have on us all in the future. On 18 October of that year the British Broadcasting Company was formed by a consortium of large firms. The BBC didn't become a corporation until 1927. The 'Company's' first general manager was John Reith, who later became the first Director General of the 'Corporation'. Reith was a tall Scot and a stickler for discipline. Though aloof, somewhat narrow-minded and dictatorial, he laid the foundations nearly sixty years ago for the broadcasting empire that is now recognised as the finest in the world.

The first broadcasting licence fee was ten shillings (50 pence). In 1922 the Company had as their headquarters Marconi House in the Strand, later moving to Savoy Hill. '2LO calling' became the signal, and the first news bulletins were read through a telephone receiver connected to a 1½ kilowatt wireless telephony receiver.

Some people were frightened of the new medium. In 1923 the Dean of Westminster refused to allow the wedding service of the Duke of York to Lady Elizabeth Bowes Lyon to be broadcast from Westminster Abbey in case it might be heard in an irreverent manner, and even by persons in a public house, with their hats on! But King George V was to be heard by 10 million people when he opened the great Wembley Exhibition in 1924. And so radio had come to stay.

Regular transmissions included solo singers and instrumentalists, poetry readings, general information, news items and church services. But it was the broadcasting of dance music that appealed to the masses and popularised radio. Outside broadcasts in the early days included Henry Hall and his Gleneagles Hotel Orchestra, Jack Payne with his Hotel Cecil Orchestra (the Hotel Cecil is now the headquarters of an oil company, situated practically next to the Savoy Hotel in the Strand). The first BBC house band was the London Radio Dance Band, directed by Sidney Firman. The first BBC dance orchestra was formed later on with Jack Payne as its leader. Of course name bands such as Roy Fox, Harry Roy, Ray Noble, Lew Stone and Ambrose were known through

George V and Queen Mary attending a charity matinée in aid of British and Foreign Sailors Society at London's Palace Theatre, May 1925. *Photograph courtesy of BBC Hulton Picture Library*

recordings played on wind-up gramophones, but it was radio that put an orchestra out in front in the twenties. John Reith tried to keep a tight rein on the amount of dance music broadcast because he was of the fervent opinion that radio should be primarily a medium for the spread of cultural and moral enlightenment. This view of Reith's was in some way perhaps directed at society, which he believed was becoming loose in its outlook. Girls, for instance, were cropping their hair short, and this was considered immoral and immodest. They were also beginning to use lipstick and make-up, which up to that time had only been associated with the stage, or women of the streets. Men were being more adventurous in their dress, wearing 'Oxford Bags' with 25-inch bottom turn-ups, or plus-fours with highly patterned sweaters, and to complete the outfit, a cap and pipe. If this was thought to be a bit too flamboyant — well, the Prince of Wales dressed like it!

The early twenties in London were creating some unusual and exciting theatre. Even a Seaside pierrot show, *The Co-optimists*, put on with a capital outlay of £900, was packing them in at the Royalty. This show produced many future star names — Davy Burnaby, Phyllis Monkman, Laddie Cliff and Stanley Holloway. Stanley could never have imagined that sixty years later he would be in the cast of the 1980 Royal Variety Performance at the age of 93.

The London Pavilion was staging the lavish C. B. Cochran revues, several of which were directed by the great André Charlot. It was Charlot and Cochran who discovered, amongst others, Jessie Matthews and Anna Neagle in the chorus line of their shows.

The audiences treated an evening at the theatre very much as an occasion then. The men were in white tie and tails, and the ladies wore all the finery they could.

One playwright who was beginning to make his presence felt was Noël Coward. Music and lyrics also came just as easily to him as had his early acting career. It was his play, *The Vortex*, that really put him on the international map.[1] Coward was to make lasting friendships within his own profession, and also within the Royal Family. In the autumn of his life he attended a wedding where Queen Elizabeth the Queen Mother and Princess Margaret were also guests. The incident is recalled by Richard Burton, and emphasises Coward's insatiable rascally wit:

> After the wedding itself, we sat down and drank champagne in this lovely garden after the Queen Mother and Princess Margaret had left, and out through the French windows came a few assorted Lords and Dukes and many Honourables, and Noël looked up, looking as someone once said of him, like a very handsome tortoise, and said, 'Here comes the riff-raff!'[2]

His knighthood was announced in the 1970 New Year honours list. Coward said, 'It was most charmingly done. I sat next to the Queen at a private luncheon, and she said, "If I offered you a knighthood would you accept it?" I said, "Of course Ma'am, I should be very honoured and very touched." I bent down to kiss her hand, disappearing from view, and Princess Margaret, who was at the other end of the table, thought I'd disappeared entirely!'

May 1926 brought the first general strike in this country. Workers of all trades backed the miners in their search for better wages and conditions, but the longer the strike dragged on the less effective became the miners' cause. They lost out in the end, and generations of mining families since have harboured the memories of those tough and uncompromising days in the mid-twenties. There were some lighter moments in 1926. The first female Channel swimmer, 18-year-old American Gertrude Ederle, made the crossing in 14½ hours. One event which went unnoticed in 1926, hardly surprisingly, was the birth of a slightly Oriental-looking boy to a Mr and Mrs James Pertwee at Amersham in Buckinghamshire. In fact I was nick-named Chung Ling Soo after a Chinese illusionist who claimed to have entertained all the crowned heads of Europe, and His Excellency the Emperor of China. I did try to trace his claims once, but I only got as far as the Grand Theatre

Doncaster when he appeared as second top of the bill to a trick cyclist from Brighton. I'm sure my mother never thought that nearly fifty years later I would have the honour and pleasure of shaking hands with the Queen of England at the 1975 Royal Variety Performance at the London Palladium.

The royal show of 1926, again at the Alhambra in the presence of the King and Queen, included the Liverpool comedian Robb Wilton and the John Tiller Dancers, a precision troupe of girls who were to grace the variety stage for many years to come. Bransby Williams portrayed Dickens characters, and the Houston Sisters, Billy Bennett and Dick Henderson, the Yorkshire comedian, father of our own respected and talented Dickie Henderson, were also in the cast. Dick Henderson would walk on in a lounge suit and bowler hat slightly too small for him, and relate stories about his domestic life and other personal events. He finished his act with an incredibly fast dance or a straight song, and was probably the first stand-up comedian to do so.

Although Jack Payne and his orchestra and other band leaders were becoming well known through the new medium of radio, the honour of being the first variety orchestra to be included in a royal performance fell to Jack Hylton and his band in this show. Hylton had started his professional career as a concert party pianist at Gorleston, near Yarmouth, and had gone on to be a song plugger on the Golden Mile at Blackpool before forming his own band. Among other publicity stunts, Jack and his band were the first to broadcast from an aeroplane flying over Blackpool during a resident season there. Later on he produced some spectacular West End shows, had a long lease on the Victoria Palace Theatre, and for years was to manage the Crazy Gang. The 1926 show was unique in that it was the first Royal Variety Performance to be broadcast.

The 1927 royal show was staged for the first time at the Victoria Palace, but it would certainly not be the last. It was attended as usual by members of the Royal Family. Taking part was Albert Whelan, an Australian entertainer who began his act whistling his signature tune, which became very popular, and at the same time removing his top hat, scarf and white gloves. At the end of his act he repeated his whistling while putting on the hat, scarf and gloves. In those days comedians and entertainers always had a style of their own, and Whelan's was particularly recognisable. Other artistes in the show included Wee Georgie Wood, a midget of a man dressed as a small boy, with Dolly Harmer playing his mother. His popularity was to last for many years. Norman Long with his amusing songs at the piano was a concert party performer turned cabaret entertainer, and was later to make a big reputation for himself on radio, as were Flotsam and Jetsam, a double act with the former at the piano. Jetsam had a bass voice and had already appeared in a royal variety show in 1921 as a solo artiste under his real name, Malcolm McEachern. Flotsam's name was B. C. Hilliam.

The London Coliseum was the venue for the Royal Variety Performance in March 1928. The King and Queen were again present. Artistes taking part were Gracie Fields, the Lancashire lass who had come to prominence in a revue called *Mr. Tower of London*. Our Gracie, as we would come to know her, had an incredible voice, ranging over several octaves, and a bouncy sense of fun and vitality. Anton Dolin and his company of dancers were in this show, along with Jack Hylton and his band, Will Hay, Noni and Horace, a musical clown act, and Stanelli and partner. Stanelli later became famous on radio and the halls with his 'Stag Party'. It was an unusual entertainment. The setting was supposed to be Stanelli's flat, where he would invite all sorts of male artistes to join him for an evening of informal parlour entertainment, and during this they would give excerpts from their usual acts and extra items between themselves. His guests would include well known comedians, singers and musical acts such as Vine, More and Nevard. In this show at the Coliseum a dame comedian made his royal début, Clarkson Rose. Rose recalls his emotions on that particular night. He wasn't on until the second half and the waiting was agonising:

> After pacing up and down the dressing room for a while I went to the stage door for some air and there was a well known Agent in the vicinity who I knew. 'Feeling a bit jumpy are you?' he said. 'I certainly am,' I replied. He said, 'Come out and have a drink, it will steady you up.' I think he must have bought me a large one, and as I was not used to drinking in any form before working it had more than a relaxed effect on me. Back in the theatre I heard the voice on the dressing room tannoy, 'Mr. Rose, you're on in five minutes.' I walked down the corridor to the stage area and heard my introductory music as if it were coming from a distance, and I walked on stage in a sort of trance. I sang my first song to only polite applause and quickly left the stage to change, ready for my second song. When I entered for that I slipped on the highly polished stage and up went my bustle, revealing my red bloomers! At the moment of the fall, Queen Mary was seen to rock with laughter, and a press photographer took a photo of her in the Royal Box which appeared in many newspapers next day. From the moment of the fall on stage I could do no wrong, but it was the first and last time I ever took a drink before a show. A leading daily commentary on the evening's entertainment said, 'Queen Mary was most amused with Clarkson Rose's delicious burlesque of a Victorian Dame, and the little trip he did, displaying voluminous underclothing caused roars of laughter led by Her Majesty.' What a bit of unexpected luck![3]

Clarkson Rose went on to become one of Britain's premier dame comedians, and in later years, with his wife Olive Fox, ran his own company called 'Twinkle', a show born at the seaside which also toured for many years all over the country. Rose gave many of today's established artistes a start in his productions. He was a stickler for discipline, but at the same time kind and humorous.

Nineteen twenty-eight saw the emergence of two lasting events in entertainment. The first talking picture arrived from America, *The Jazz Singer*, starring Al Jolson. It was in this film that he spoke the immortal line, 'You ain't heard nothin' yet.' And we certainly hadn't. Jolson followed this up with *The Singing Fool*, and the talkies were established. They started a revolution, with the public flocking to see their film idols talking on the screen. Theatre managements were predicting that this was going to finish live entertainment — it had barely survived the silent movies but could it compete with sound as well? Two people who thought it could were George Black, on the board of directors running the London Palladium Theatre, and his booking manager, Val Parnell, son of a famous ventriloquist, Fred Russell. The Palladium had gone through a period of mixed fortunes during its existence, but Black and Parnell believed that straightforward variety at the theatre would do well, and in 1928 they launched their first big variety bill, with Gracie Fields, Billy Bennett, a playlet starring Ivor Novello and Phyllis Monkman, one of the original Co-optimists, and supporting artistes. As the late Bill Boorne wrote, 'George Black and Val Parnell found the stars, and the public found the Palladium.' This new policy was to prosper during the thirties when it was to become the best known theatre in the world, and would very soon be staging the first of many Royal Variety performances.

Another turning-point in cinematic history in 1928 was the showing in cartoon form of a little mouse called Mickey created by Walt Disney. This Disney cartoon was based on the exploits of the American aviation pioneer Colonel Lindbergh, and was called 'Plane Crazy'. Mickey Mouse, with windswept hair in the style of Lindbergh, tries to impress his girl-friend Minnie Mouse by taking her up in his home-made aeroplane, with hilarious consequences. Mickey was later joined by Donald Duck, Goofy and other characters. Children and grown-ups soon became addicts of the adventures of these funny little animals. Of course this was just the start for Disney, who later created full-length cartoons such as *Snow White and the Seven Dwarfs, Pinocchio* and *Fantasia*.

There was no royal performance in 1929 due to the illness of George V. After this illness he went to convalesce at Bognor Regis. When asked how he liked it, he was reputed to have said, 'Oh bugger Bognor.' If he did say it, I am sure there must have been a good reason!

The twenties went out with the disastrous Wall Street crash in the United States in 1929. This was to affect not only Americans but also economies throughout the world. Thousands of businesses, large and small, went bankrupt overnight; suicides by those who had lost everything in the crash were commonplace. What would the thirties hold for the world of entertainment? It was certainly going to be exciting, but the national and international events of this decade were to overshadow all else.

Notes

1. Noël Coward's achievements and life's work have been covered by various authors, notably in a splendid book, *Noël*, by Charles Castle, which was the basis of the television production *Noël* (Book Club Associates and W. H. Allen, 1973).
2. Ibid.
3. Extract from Clarkson Rose, *Red Plush and Greasepaint* (Museum Press, 1964).

4

THE UMBRELLA MAN

The 1930 Royal Variety Performance at the London Palladium was the first to be staged at this great theatre and was a tribute to the hard work and flair of George Black and Val Parnell, whose new policy of high-speed variety was paying off at the Palladium. George V and Queen Mary saw a glittering royal show on that occasion. The programme included Tom Payne and Vera Hilliard, a comedy double act based on Napoleon's march across the Alps. This was a situation piece of burlesque comedy sending up Napoleon's known historical dialogue. Every now and again Tom Payne would reach into his pocket for a handful of paper pieces, throw them into the air and say, 'Oh the snow, the snow,' etc. It was all very simple comedy but very effective. This type of act was later revived by Billy Revel and Pat Fields. Gillie Potter, who was also in this show, was different from the broader variety act of the time and this probably restricted his appeal to the more conventional music-hall audience. He became a big radio personality whose opening line on the air was, 'Good evening England, this is Gillie Potter here, speaking to you in English.' This opening was, I believe, his way of countering the assortment of accents used by comedy artistes at that time — Cockney, Jewish, foreign tongues in varying degrees and pseudo 'Oxford'. Potter's accent was certainly cultured but quite genuine. His comedy routines were centred around the happenings of his native village of 'Hogsnorton'. Apart from his entertaining abilities Potter was also a great authority on heraldry. He retired to Bournemouth where he died fairly recently in his eighties. Will Hay, fast becoming a star with the schoolmaster character he was portraying, was also in the show at the Palladium. He was the man of authority hanging on to his position by a whisker. He had cheeky pupils as his comedy stooges who always got the better of him, but only after a battle of wits in the classroom. Hay would get out of a tight corner by giving some ridiculous answers to questions posed by himself to the pupils, and if they didn't believe him he would just say, 'Oh shut up, boys, and let's get on with the next question.' Will Hay was a very keen astronomer, and could probably have made a career in that field had he wanted to. He built his own observatory, which is still standing and can be seen quite clearly by the side of the A1 road approaching Mill Hill going north out of London.

The highly competitive cinema entertainment was now beginning to gather momentum. Large picture houses were being built in major towns, many of them with sizeable and ornate organs which used to play when you entered the cinema. Just before the programme started the giant machine, organist atop and bathed in illumination of changing colours, would slowly submerge into its well of darkness. In between the films up would come the organist, turning to smile at the audience and acknowledge the applause, before going into a medley of well trodden melodies and finally disappearing once more into the bowels of the stage, while your ears were shattered by the MGM lion roaring its introduction to the 'Big Picture'. The curtains would part, revealing the lion in all his glory as the lights went down and courting couples cuddled up closer with their chocolates. The organists' popularity grew with the expansion of the film business and many of those who were featured in broadcasts direct from the larger cinemas became household names.

It was George V who, in 1931, quickly saw the value of theatre in combating the depression. Noël Coward's *Cavalcade* was playing at the Theatre Royal Drury Lane at the time. This was a historical musical review of the past greatnesses of Britain with a message of good times to come again as its closing theme. King George and Queen Mary took their whole family to see Coward's musical the day after the General Election and made the unofficial visit a platform for a show of patriotism, confirming Coward's belief that there would be good times ahead. The royal party were greeted inside and outside the theatre with enormous enthusiasm and loyalty.

The Brighton seaside comedian Harry Sargant was in one royal show of the early thirties; but by then he had changed his name to Max Miller. With his multi-coloured plus-four suit, white Homburg hat, co-respondent shoes and cheeky line in patter, he established an instant rapport with the audience. Billy Bennett had teamed up temporarily with James Carew to do a black-faced act known as Alexander and Mose, a partnership they had established on radio in a show called the Kentucky Minstrels produced by Harry S. Pepper, the son of a famous seaside show proprietor, Will Pepper. The Kentucky Minstrels were based on the minstrel shows popular on the beaches at the turn of the century and before. It was the growing popularity of radio that quickly helped to establish performers who otherwise would have taken far longer to emerge, because of course they were playing to a far wider audience. The difference in those days was that performers who made their names on radio nearly always had a good theatre background and so were quite at home when they became bill-toppers as a result of their appearance on the air. Nowadays it is sometimes more difficult, because many artistes start off in television and find the theatre too big a medium to cope with when they are thrust into playing major theatre venues direct from 'the box'.

Other royal performers at this time were illusionist Jasper Maskelyne and a young song and dance man, Jack Buchanan, whose first Royal Variety Performance was at the Palladium in 1932. Buchanan was to become a big musical comedy star in such shows as *Stand Up and Sing, Mr. Whittington, Toni* and *That's A Good Girl*. He also produced many of his stage successes, and his films were enormously popular, none more so than *Bandwaggon*, in which he co-starred with Fred Astaire. His leading ladies included Anna Neagle, Elsie Randolph and Jeanette MacDonald. Some of the songs he sang still have a great style about them today — 'And her Mother Came Too', 'Goodnight Vienna', 'Now that I've Found You', 'There's Always Tomorrow' and 'Who' were among his big successes. His voice was unmistakable and perhaps unique in its way.

Two men in a comedy double act making their début in the royal show of 1932 were destined to become the undisputed court jesters to the monarchy — Bud Flanagan and Chesney Allen. Nervo and Knox, the eccentric comedy dancers, were to perform a burlesque ballet in the show. It was decided by George Black and Bud Flanagan to do a straight ballet sequence before the burlesque with a commentary by Chesney Allen, with Bud doing the commentary for the Nervo and Knox comedy send-up of it. Nervo and Knox were brilliant in their routine and every line of Flanagan's spoken commentary got huge laughs from the audience. This was the beginning of the talented Crazy Gang, later to be joined by Naughton and Gold, Carryl and Munday, Eddie Gray and, for a time, Tommy Trinder. There was, however, a small drama in Flanagan and Allen's first show in the presence of their monarch. In the interval George V sent for George Black and asked him what time the show would finish. Black, knowing the show was going well and that the King was thoroughly enjoying it, said, 'About eleven o'clock, Sir.' The King was a stickler for time and made it known he would like it to finish a little earlier, as he didn't want the police lining the route back to Buckingham Palace to be too late on duty. The staff at the Palace were also waiting up for their majesties' return. Black of course complied with the King's wishes, and went back-stage to make the necessary cuts to get the show down on time. Flanagan and Allen, who were doing their own spot towards the end of the show, were asked to shorten their routine, which they did, leaving them with just one song. The royal party left exactly at the time they had wanted to. Flanagan said, 'Although it was a great disappointment for us to cut, we had appeared in our first royal show.' A chance exuberant 'off the cuff' gesture by Bud Flanagan during the final afternoon rehearsal of the show is still used nowadays at the end of the performance: 'Rehearsing the National Anthem, we were told to turn half left and face the Royal Box. After the Anthem was sung, I impulsively shouted, "Hip-Hip" and the rest of the company of 150 shouted "Hurrah" three times.'[1] George Black asked Bud to keep it in for the actual performance, and his involuntary action that afternoon has become a ritual to be followed at the end of all Royal Variety performances since.

The Crazy Gang were to become almost resident at the Palladium. The comedy antics of the gang depended on the inventiveness of them all, but the success of their popularity was due very largely to the warm personality of Bud Flanagan and his team mate Chesney Allen. Later a wider public became aware of their ability through the songs they wrote and sang together. One of them, 'The Umbrella Man', was a typically catchy song inspired by the famous brolly Neville Chamberlain was seen holding on his return from Munich.

Although there had been warlike rumblings during the middle of this decade nobody took them very seriously, and Britain, like most of the world, wanted to get on with the business of enjoying all the new innovations and discoveries that were being presented to them. After all, it was far more exciting to read in the *Picture-goer* or *Picture-show* about the intimate private lives of the idols of the celluloid screen, such as Clark Gable, Carole Lombard and Charles Laughton.

The 1933 Royal Performance audience was entertained by one of the simplest acts ever to appear on a stage, yet one that became a legend in the theatre, Wilson, Kepple and Betty. Their act, which never changed, depicted a couple of Middle Eastern gents, complete with fezes, straight out of the casbah, and a girl doing an eccentric sand dance. They were a speciality act that fitted into any music-hall bill, and didn't clash with anyone. The booking departments of the theatres knew exactly what they did and what they needed in the way of stage settings. Wilson and Kepple never changed, but they did have several different 'Bettys', either because they were getting married or having children, or just simply that they'd had enough sand in their shoes. In fact one particular Betty took over from her mother in the act.

Billy Bennett was now at the top of the comedy tree, his reputation being firmly established through radio, the music hall and smoking concerts. He had a ridiculous goon-like approach to comedy. His dress was absurd: he wore a shabby tail suit, loose-fitting collar and big boots, and his sparse hair was combed across his forehead in a quiff. His bill matter was 'Almost a Gentleman'. He was popular with pretty well everyone in the social scale, and I remember my own father, who had a reasonably mature and sophisticated sense of humour, being a terrific radio fan of Billy Bennett's. Bennett's style of comedy was popular with George V, who had always preferred the buffoonery of artistes like Harry Tate, Will Hay or George Robey to the more sophisticated type of humour. In fact this was the main reason the King liked music hall, and Billy Bennett certainly was very much of that medium. He was mainly famous for his nonsensical monologues which were parodies of well known pieces, and very funny they were too. John Fisher sets out Bennett's parody of the 'Green Eye of the Little Yellow God', which was, as far as Bennett was concerned, 'The Tale of the Green Tie of the Little Yellow Dog'. His booming, rather fruity voice would proclaim:

There's a cock-eyed yellow poodle to the North of gonga pooch,
There's a little hot cross bun that's turning green,
There's a double jointed wop-wop doing trucks in who-flung-dung,
And you're a better man that I am Gunga-Din. [2]

I wonder how many people know, I certainly didn't, that gonga pooch is a colloquialism for 'arseholes'. George V, being a naval man, certainly did, and with his knowledge of the slang would have been one of the few in the audience to appreciate the joke.

If the Crazy Gang had made the London Palladium almost their second home, that theatre had, through the hard work of George Black, Val Parnell, Harry Marlow and their associates, become the home of the Royal Variety Performance.

The wedding of the King's youngest son, George, Duke of Kent, to the lovely Princess Marina of Greece, in 1934, was a welcome chance for people to show just how much they could enjoy the pageantry of a royal occasion, and perhaps it was just what was wanted at the time. A one-act play was included in the performance that year, an item that was fairly rare but not totally new to the productions. This one featured British actor Cedric Hardwicke, later Sir Cedric after he had made a name for himself in Hollywood. The playlet was called *The Carrier Pigeon*. The mind boggles at the thought of its content and the part Hardwicke played in the piece. Jack Hylton and his band were in a royal show at the Palladium and Hylton in that performance introduced a surprise item which included boxer Jimmy Wilde, footballer Alex James (he of the long shorts), and triple Wimbledon tennis champion Fred Perry, who now commentates during the Wimbledon fortnight. There was also the first appearance in a royal performance of an American artiste, the Red Hot Momma, Sophie Tucker. Elsie and Doris Waters in the guise of 'Gert and Daisy' brought their relaxed style of domestic humour to the proceedings, a style that was to prove so successful for many years after. Their brother was the much loved and respected Jack Warner of television's *Dixon of Dock Green* fame. Preceding the Waters sisters in this royal show were Arthur Lucan and Kitty McShane. They were husband and wife, but on stage Arthur Lucan played 'Old Mother Riley', in drag of course, and Kitty, his 'daughter'. They became huge names in entertainment not only on stage and radio but also in films. Their comedy situations in the latter medium still hold up today. In this royal performance they did their famous crockery smashing act. Old Mother Riley in her annoyance at Kitty's behaviour in the home starts to throw cups, saucers and plates in all directions until the stage is littered with broken china, but there is one plate that refuses to break and this gives scope for some outrageous antics of frustration from Old Mother Riley. Altogether a brilliant performance by Lucan, and of course the last plate does finally break to roars of laughter from the audience, and on this occasion from King George too, who was seen to be almost helpless with laughter in the Royal Box. It is worth mentioning that while all the broken china was being collected after this scene, Elsie and Doris Waters were doing their spot in a front cloth, and perhaps less experienced performers would have been put off by the sound of the shattered china being swept up behind the cloth. The whole show really was variety *par excellence* to present before the King and Queen.

It was gratifying for George V and Queen Mary to see the enormous show of loyalty accorded to them in 1935 on the occasion of their Silver Jubilee. The celebrations went on for several weeks in cities, towns and hamlets. Street parties were organised with an abundance of food and pop for the youngsters, and pianos were commandeered to perch on the pavement and play for dancing for the adults which went on far into the night. Drinking mugs, plates, dishes, biscuit tins and other items were produced with their majesties' pictures on them — now collectors' items. The Jubilee procession through London was blessed with blue skies and sunshine, and I remember my brother John (not to be confused with cousin Jon of Worzel Gummidge and Dr Who fame) going up to London very early in the morning to gain his vantage point, complete with his 5s (25p) Box Brownie camera. He did come back with one or two very good photos, although how he was able to photograph anything in the midst of, in my brother's words, 'millions of people who seemed to have filled every pavement and viewpoint for the great occasion' was a mystery. The Jubilee Royal Performance at the Palladium was in doubt at one time due to the King's health, but he improved and His Majesty attended the show, together with Queen Mary, the Duchess of York and the Dowager Countess of Airlie. The show included Sandy

THE LONDON PALLADIUM

OXFORD CIRCUS, W.

General Theatre Corporation, Ltd.
Managing Director:
MARK OSTRER

Direction:
GEORGE BLACK
Resident Manager: C. RHODES PARRY

'Phone GERRARD 7373

6.30 | TWICE NIGHTLY commencing AUG. 12th, 1935 **MATINEES** AT **2.30** WEDNESDAY & THURSDAY | **9.0**

FOR TWO WEEKS ONLY   (FIRST WEEK)

GRACIE FIELDS

CHEVALIER BROS
ACROBATIC HUMOUR

JUGGLING MELVILLES

MITO TRIO
Novelty Equilibrists

FOUR
America's Sensational Skaters

WILL FYFFE

WARD AND VAN

GENE SHELDON
With LORETTA FISCHER

WHIRLWINDS
FIRST TIME HERE

RAY HULING AND SEAL
FIRST TIME HERE

SENATOR MURPHY

VENITA GOULD

Scotland's Representative Character Comedian

The Political Humorist

AMERICA'S FOREMOST IMPERSONATOR

COMMENCING TUESDAY AUG. 27TH | OUR NEW PRODUCTION "ROUND ABOUT REGENT STREET" PRODUCED BY GEORGE BLACK | BOX OFFICE NOW OPEN

Variety bill, London Palladium, 1935. *By courtesy of Moss Empires Ltd*

Powell ('Can you hear me mother!') in a sketch called 'The Test Match', and Sandy must have been the first comedian to parody the noble game on stage. Sandy told me that he got dressed for that royal show at 2.30 in the afternoon, and walked about all day going from one person to another asking the time. The show didn't start until 8 p.m., so poor Sandy, dressed in cricket gear, complete with pads, sweater and boots, got hotter and hotter as the day wore on. Hot or not, Sandy hit the audience for six on the night.

Little did the public know that this would be George V's last attendance at a Royal Variety Performance. He had done the music hall proud over the years with his patronage, and I'm sure he would have agreed that the music hall had given him an enormous amount of pleasure during his reign. Probably the most dramatic radio broadcast up to that time was heard on 19 January 1936: 'The King's life is moving peacefully to its close.' Although most people in the country had realised the King was ill, his death stunned the nation.

Edward VIII came to the throne with all the goodwill of the country behind him. He had been the people's Prince, and they hoped he would be the people's King. We will never know whether or not he would have been. The country itself was changing and people were becoming more adventurous in their outlook. New housing estates were springing up around the capital and you could buy a nice little semi-detached for £300. The owner-occupier was emerging in the lower income bracket. It was *everyone* for tennis in the suburbs, probably because the game had been glamorised by the Wimbledon success of Fred Perry, 'Bunny' Austin and Suzanne Longlen. Hobbs and Sutcliffe, Hammond and Bradman were the schoolboy cricketing heroes. Soccer was frowned upon by some public schools, although the man on the terraces was quite happy with it, and King George V had regularly presided over the annual Cup Final at Wembley. It was a time of breakfast with Shredded Wheat and Force (you could send away a coupon for a 'Sunny Jim' doll, the symbol of the cereal). Walls, famous for sausages, had gone into the ice cream business in a big way. Three-wheel ice-box vehicles were pedalled through the streets in their hundreds by smartly uniformed salesmen selling bricks, tubs and snowfruits, the equivalent of today's iced lollies. Notices on the vehicles said, 'Stop me and buy one.'

Edward VIII had little time during his short reign to be involved with the theatre, but as Prince of Wales during the twenties and thirties he spent his leisure hours relaxing in various night clubs frequented by his friends — the Kit Kat, Ciro's and Quaglino's. The Embassy, probably the most popular, boasted Ambrose and his Band and the dance hostess was Queenie Thompson, who had started her career as a soubrette in

Edwin Adeler's Concert Party and later changed her name to Merle Oberon and became a Hollywood film star. The Prince would sometimes invite the cabaret performers back to his London residence, York House, at the end of an evening in the club for some informal entertainment. Among his favourites were Layton and Johnston and Hutch, very popular in this country at that time, and the first black entertainers to be honoured with a private command, as it were. Ambrose, Roy Fox, Joe Loss, Ray Noble, Harry Roy, Carrol Gibbons, Lew Stone and others were now the popular names in the nighteries. Some of their instrumentalists, like George Chisholm, Ted Heath, Sid Phillips, Stanley Black and Nat Gonella, later formed their own combinations. A vocalist who sang with many of them and was a star in his own right was Al Bowley, who might have reached great heights had he not been killed by enemy action in 1941. Many generations since have heard this great artiste on record; in fact he has become something of a cult. You might have heard his voice, along with other musicians of that time, in the recent television serial *Pennies from Heaven*.

As far as his theatre-going was concerned, Edward VIII when Prince of Wales liked to keep it at an official level. Ex-television producer Albert Stevenson recalled an incident when he was call boy at the Alhambra Theatre of varieties in the late twenties. He had to stand on the prompt side of the stage during the performances, and one of his duties was to stop anyone coming through the pass door from the auditorium while the show was in progress, even the King of England. One night there

HRH The Prince of Wales (later Edward VIII) opening the Shakespeare Memorial Theatre, Stratford-on-Avon, April 1932, being greeted by Miss Scott who designed the theatre. *Photograph courtesy of Hulton Picture Library*

was a knock on the pass door and as usual Albert said, 'I'm sorry, you can't come through here.' A voice from the other side said, 'I'm the Prince of Wales.' Albert said, 'Sorry, Sir, you'll have to go round to the Stage Door,' and he refused to let the Prince through. After some deliberation and consultation with the manager, George Reynolds, the Prince was allowed through. He asked Albert to hold his small dog while he went upstairs to see the Houston Sisters, Renée and Billie, who were on the bill. The dog, probably through nerves, wet Albert's immaculately pressed trousers. When the Prince later heard about this he asked to have the cleaning bill sent to him. Later in the week a guardsman arrived at the Stage Door of the Alhambra bearing a ten-shilling note for Albert for looking after the dog. The Prince also sent a note to George Reynolds saying he thought young Stevenson ought to have a rise for doing his 'guard' duty properly at the pass door. Young Albert got a five-shilling rise from Mr Reynolds on command of the Prince. Albert Stevenson went on to become one of our most distinguished television producers both with the BBC and ATV, and was responsible for the long-running series *New Faces*.

Cicely Courtneidge recalls in her book *Cicely* that at the beginning of the thirties she and her husband Jack Hulbert were in a series of revues at the 'Little Theatre'.

> The Prince of Wales with the Duke of Gloucester and the Duke of Kent paid several visits to that theatre. The Duke of Gloucester, who had a high pitched laugh you could not miss, found the show very funny and usually sat with a handkerchief crammed in front of his mouth to try to control his laughter.[3]

The Prince of Wales was in a box on an unofficial visit to the London Hippodrome on one occasion when Harry Lauder was in the show and the Prince was really enjoying the atmosphere of the evening. Rumours at that time were rife as to his possible involvement with a certain lady. As Harry Lauder was finishing his act the Prince called out together with the audience, 'I Love a Lassie, Harry.' Lauder looked up at the Prince and said, 'Yes, I know you do, but we all want to know who she is.' The Prince of Wales took this very well and laughed with the rest of the audience.

In the thirties Henry Sherek, who not only produced various stage shows but also the more intimate style of cabaret entertainment, was engaged by the Ritz Hotel in London to produce their floor show. One particular production was in the form of a French café. Sherek had engaged two pianists he had seen playing in Vienna in the Kaiser Kaffee called Rawicz and Landauer. He brought them over to the Ritz and while they were playing there Sherek received a telephone call from the British Legation in Vienna — 'The Prince of Wales is giving a party at the Legation next Monday and wants you to send over Rawicz and Landauer.' 'There are plenty of double piano acts in Vienna,' he replied, 'and why deprive my customers of a very popular turn, besides you'll be saving the fares.' The Legation would not take no for an answer, saying the Prince had seen the pianists at the Ritz and would Sherek lay out the fares and send them to Vienna. Sherek treated this request as a Royal Command. He never did get the money from the Legation for the fares.[4]

Early in the thirties the Prince of Wales attended a performance at the Covent Garden Opera House in celebration of the twenty-fifth anniversary of the Royal Automobile Club. It was in the nature of a Command Performance, as the artistes had been chosen by the Prince himself and the management of the RAC. Clarkson Rose said:

> The show started at ten-thirty at night, being preceded by a huge banquet on the stage, in full view of the audience. It was a wonderful programme, and certainly more carefree than most Royal occasions. I was honoured to be included along with Harry Tate, Nellie Wallace, Albert Whelan, Georgie Wood, Will Hay and many others. The Prince of Wales had to leave earlier than expected so one or two acts did not actually perform.[5]

Of course they were disappointed, but 'they were handsomely compensated, when they received, as we all did, an evening dress cigarette case, engraved with the Royal Coat of Arms. The ladies had silver powder boxes.'[6]

In 1936 Noël Coward's *Tonight at Eight-thirty* was playing at the Phoenix Theatre in Charing Cross Road, and consisted of several one-act plays including *Still Life*, which, re-titled *Brief Encounter*, became an enormously successful film starring Trevor Howard and Celia Johnson. Shortly after the London opening Noël received word from Buckingham Palace that King Edward VIII would like seats for one of the performances. Coward continues the story:

> I was of course delighted he wanted to come, but word didn't reach me till late in the afternoon, and he wanted seats for himself and his party for that evening's performance. The Theatre was booked solidly for weeks ahead. I asked some friends of mine who were coming to the show to give up their seats, which they kindly did. The King came, and afterwards went backstage to Gertie Lawrence's dressing room and spent half an hour with her. To my astonishment he left the theatre without so much as thanking me for the seats. As I happened to be the author, the star and the producer of the show, I thought it rather ill-mannered of him and got word through letting him know. Tell him, I said, that he may be the King of England, but I'm the

Noël Coward and Gertrude Lawrence in the series of one-act plays *Tonight at 8.30* at the Phoenix Theatre, 1936. *By courtesy of The Raymond Mander & Joe Mitchenson Theatre Collection*

King of the Theatre and I expect him to respect me as such. The reply he
sent back was 'Tell Noël Coward to go and . . . . himself.' I took my hat
off to him for that, he managed to knock me down a peg or two.[7]

The King had to feel comfortable in the presence of stage folk. For
instance he was fairly outspoken about homosexuality, of which the
legitimate theatre has always had its fair share, and for years was very
cool towards Noël Coward and Somerset Maugham, both of whom he
met on various social occasions, and witty as they were, he never
completely accepted them in the early days. He called homosexuals in
general 'those fellows who fly in over the transom'.[8] Later, however,
when he was still Prince of Wales, he and Coward became friends, but
then who couldn't be friends with the witty Noël? The Prince's early
prejudice obviously disappeared, since in 1950, when he was Duke of
Windsor, he took himself a jester, one Jimmy Donahue, an outrageous
'gay' American playboy and work-shy extrovert. The fact that the
Duchess of Windsor had met Donahue and was very quickly won over
by him may have influenced the Duke in this. Jimmy Donahue was the
grandson of F. W. Woolworth, founder of the threepenny and sixpenny
High Street stores, and this was reason enough not to work, let alone the
fifteen million dollars he had been left in his grandfather's will. Donahue
could fly a plane, play the piano well and was a continual wisecracker,
which made him desirable company at parties and receptions. He had
such charm and bonhomie that he completely captivated the Windsors
and he eventually travelled back to Paris with them in the fifties after the
New York season at the Duke's invitation.

The Duke of Windsor's first visit to the theatre in Britain since his
abdication was to see *Witness for the Prosecution* at the Winter Garden
Theatre in December 1953. The crowd outside the theatre on that
evening certainly let him know he was still very much in their thoughts.
The Duke's link with the world of entertainment will probably be with
us for some time to come. We have already seen the play *Crown
Matrimonial*, which portrays the abdication crisis, and millions have
watched *Edward and Mrs Simpson* on television.

The British people had been shaken to the core by the abdication. I
vividly remember King Edward's farewell speech. My mother cried for
several hours and had to be consoled by my father who said simply,
'Well, it's his choice,' which was probably what most people thought.
Although 1936 was a somewhat sad year in the life of the British
monarchy, there was a happy event on Christmas Day with the birth to
the Duchess of Kent of a baby girl, Princess Alexandra, who has grown
up to become one of the Royal Family's most popular members. I
remember my mother's excitement on that festive night in 1936 when

we heard the good news. I know that it gave my uncle, who was enjoying the Christmas party, a chance to renew his attack on the bottle of Scotch. Our game of Monopoly was frequently interrupted by my uncle's announcement of cheers and good health to the new Princess. Little did I imagine that one day the lovely princess would almost catch me with my trousers down in a theatre dressing-room!

On the first night of his reign George VI said to his cousin, Lord Louis Mountbatten, 'Dickie, this is terrible. I never wanted this to happen. I'm quite unprepared for it. David [the ex-King] has been trained for this all his life.'[9] Well, unprepared or not, and of course he was not, the new King became loved and respected by his peoples. A great amount of the credit for the affection that developed between King George and his subjects must go to his wife and Queen, Elizabeth. She steadied what must have been a very difficult first few months for them both. Apart from anything else, they had to re-establish the monarchy. Their great strength lay within themselves as a family. Perhaps unknowingly, they epitomised the sort of family unit that made up a large part of the social structure of this country at that time.

When time allowed, the King and Queen, with their two daughters, liked to go down to the small Royal Lodge at Windsor, with as little staff around them as possible, and relax in the garden, which they planned and worked in themselves.

Their majesties' Coronation in May 1937 was a moment for everyone to pledge allegiance to the King and Queen. It was a huge show of confidence in them, and I'm sure that King George and Queen Elizabeth never forgot this. Patronage by the Royal Family of the theatre continued.

Three great-grandchildren of Queen Victoria, the Duke of Kent, the Marquess of Milford Haven and Lord Louis Mountbatten were present at the Lyric Theatre on 21 June 1937 for the historic first-night presentation of Laurence Housman's hitherto banned play, *Victoria Regina*. It was apparently felt that a hundred years after the Queen's accession to the throne the sacredness of her character had sufficiently diminished.[10]

The Coronation year Royal Variety Performance in November at the London Palladium was a glittering affair. Those taking part were Will Fyfe, Cicely Courtneidge, Florence Desmond, a brilliant impressionist who really was an international star, Ethel Revnell and Gracie West, a popular female double act at that time, Max Miller and Norman Evans, whose gossipy lady 'over the garden wall' was very funny indeed. Evans was not only an established top of the bill, but an extremely kind man, and was loved by all those who worked with him. George Formby, who was making his first and only Royal Variety appearance in London, was

Harry Tate and his son Ronnie performing their motorbike sketch which was included in an early television transmission from Alexandra Palace, 1937. *Photograph courtesy of Ronnie Tate*

later to become one of the biggest box office attractions, not only on stage but in films as well. Formby was a brilliant exponent of the ukelele and his records sold in millions. His approach to everything he did was simple in its content. He was never vulgar, and in fact this lad from Lancashire was rather naïve and coy as a person. Another Lancastrian in the show, making her third Royal Variety appearance, was Gracie Fields. The Crazy Gang were as funny as ever all dressed up as elderly female flower sellers around Eros's statue in Piccadilly. The real ladies were a feature of the London scene for many years. The royal show was of course attended by King George VI and Queen Elizabeth in the first year of their reign, accompanied by the Duke and Duchess of Kent. The royal party obviously enjoyed themselves, laughing as loudly as anybody in the theatre that night. Janet Flanner remembers: 'The Royal brothers smoked cigarettes, the Royal ladies helped themselves to chocolates, and all four joined Gracie Fields in singing the chorus of "Sally".'[11]

If you talk to anybody about the nervous months leading up to the last war, most people would automatically think of 1939, but for my family, and others I'm sure, it started in 1938. Nearly everyone believed we were on the brink of a terrible catastrophe. Everything you read in the newspapers or heard on the radio pointed to it. Rearmament was well under way, air raid shelters were being designed, and young men were enthusiastically telling one another that they wouldn't wait to be called up in an emergency, they would volunteer, particularly young men who had been fired by the adventurous aviators of the thirties. My eldest brother held this view. Naturally parents who had eligible sons were worried at the prospect. Believe it or not, my great memory of 1938 was listening to a cricket commentary with my father, which I can remember practically word for word to this day. It was the occasion of the last Test Match at the Oval between England and Australia, when Len Hutton wrote his name in to the sporting record books, scoring 364 runs, beating Donald Bradman's previous best 334, made at Leeds in 1934.

A silly little man with glasses, who sang about bees and punctures, and a tall, lean, rather well spoken gentleman made a big impact through the medium of radio in 1938. They were Arthur Askey and Richard Murdoch, in a situation comedy series, *Bandwaggon*, the first of its kind in this country. Both Askey and Murdoch have remained stars ever since. I know Arthur and Dickie, and they both deserve their successes, which span more then fifty years. Few people knew that the 1938 Royal Variety Performance at the London Coliseum in November had its hair-raising moments behind the scenes. The show included Richard Hearne, who later was to create the slapstick character 'Mr Pastry'. Also appearing were the two Leslies, Holmes and Sarony. Leslie Sarony, who wrote the songs and is still writing them today, is a marvellous entertainer and in recent years has been making a name for himself as a straight actor. The back-stage drama I was talking about concerned the show *Me and My Girl*, which was then in residence at the Victoria Palace Theatre. There was to be an excerpt from the production at the Coliseum in the royal show and the scenery had to be taken apart, taken over to the Coliseum and re-assembled in time for the performance. Staff worked all day and it was ready with just a few minutes to spare. *Me and My Girl* starred Lupino Lane (the Lupinos have been an incredible family, with their treasures of comedy and theatrical inventiveness). The big number from the show was 'The Lambeth Walk', a song and dance production that is still popular today at family parties and social occasions large and small, high-brow or low-brow. On the night the revolving stage started to go round the wrong way and instead of bringing Lupino Lane on to lead the company into the Lambeth Walk it started to take him off. However, it was quickly put to rights. For the Royal Performance the Victoria Palace chorus was augmented by practically every well known stage artiste at that time, in all some 250. If this was to be the last Royal Variety Performance for some time the 'Lambeth Walk' certainly sent the audience and the royal party home in a happy frame of mind on that November evening.

I remember spending my pocket money in 1938 on George Formby

George VI and Queen Elizabeth attending a performance of *Me and My Girl* at the Victoria Palace Theatre, 1 May 1939. *From the Illustrated London News, by courtesy of Theatre Museum*

Regal Zonophone records. I think I had the set of them which I subsequently played on my aunt's prized radiogram (they were pretty rare in those days) until they were almost worn smooth. Even my aunt, who was something of a high-brow, reluctantly began to take to George's warm and friendly style.

Early in 1939 the first commercial transatlantic service was begun by Pan American Airways' 'Yankee Clipper' — New York, Bermuda, the Azores, Lisbon, Bordeaux, Marseilles and Southampton. It wasn't to last long, not because of any inefficiency in the service, but because of one man's desire for world dominance.

On the morning of 1 September 1939 I was wakened by my mother, who told me that an aunt, yes, the same one I had plagued with my collection of George Formby 78s, had phoned to say that obviously war was imminent and that she thought we all ought to go to her house in the country in case the expected bombing started in London. We were staying with another aunt in south-east London at the time, and my cousins and I, in a fury of excitement and packing, rushed around chattering like demented canaries. In the hot afternoon we were driven down to a little village called West Chiltington in Sussex. There were other more organised exits from the capital and most main line stations were coping with these. We settled into our new environment very quickly and if this was what war was all about, well, we were going to enjoy it, and anyway it would all be over by Christmas. On 3 September we all went to church and came back to my aunt's house where my uncle told us, and several more friends and relatives who seemed to be joining the household during that weekend, that the Prime Minister was to make an important announcement on the radio at eleven o'clock. It was a lovely sunny morning, and everyone crowded round the wireless. Neville Chamberlain, in a faltering and emotional voice, said, 'We are at war with Germany.' While the grown-ups walked about in silent groups, and we kids enquired as to whether Aunt Amy had made another apple and blackberry pie for lunch, the atmosphere was shattered by an air-raid siren. Everybody dashed about, telling each other to come indoors and 'sit still'. Uncle reassured us all that West Chiltington was of no military value, that he didn't even think Hitler knew where it was, and that the siren was probably all a mistake. Which, as it happens, it was. A lone single-seater monoplane had got caught up in the new and rather confused early warning system as it crossed the coast that morning. Nevertheless we had been shaken into realising that life from now on was going to be different.

The government immediately ordered all theatres, cinemas and other meeting-places where people were likely to congregate in large numbers to be closed, at least for the time being. Only public houses were given a reprieve, as it was thought they might be good for morale. We seemed to listen to the radio all day. The BBC was the voice of sanity, giving us instructions for this and that, telling us how we could grow our own food and how fresh home baking could be carried out without wastage. It wasn't only mothers and children who had been evacuated from the cities into rural Britain: the BBC was evacuated to Bristol, Llandudno and other far-flung places, although at the time nobody knew where, for security reasons, and only a skeleton staff remained in London to read the news.

At this point a comedy programme came on to the scene that is still remembered today — *It's That Man Again*, *ITMA*, starring Tommy Handley with Jack Train, Derek Guyler and a whole host of people who became legendary through the characters they created — 'Mrs Mopp', 'Senior S-So', 'Funf', 'Claude and Cecil' and many others. Tommy Handley himself was superb, and this one-time concert party and music-hall comedian from Liverpool became as famous as Sir Winston Churchill and Adolf Hitler. *ITMA* was not only recorded from BBC studios but also from naval bases, army camps and Windsor Castle. The programme was very popular with the King and Queen, and as a result the show was invited to broadcast from there. In the first few inactive months of the war it was stalemate in the theatre, but gradually they were given the chance to open again. The first was the Windmill Theatre, which had only been closed for a week or so, and was a big attraction for the many servicemen from all parts of the world who were waiting for the balloon to go up. At least most of us had a peaceful Christmas in this country in 1939, and we felt that in George VI we had a monarch who would help us through what difficulties might lie ahead. He understood our apprehensions and fears. In listening to the King's Christmas Day broadcast we were convinced he wouldn't let us down. How right we were.

Notes

1. Bud Flanagan, *My Crazy Life* (New English Library, 1962).
2. John Fisher, *Funny Way to be a Hero* (first published Frederick Muller, 1973; Paladin, 1976).
3. Cicely Courtneidge, *Cicely* (Hutchinson, 1953).
4. Henry Sherek, *Not in Front of the Children* (Heinemann, 1959).
5. Clarkson Rose, *Red Plush and Greasepaint* (Museum Press, 1964).
6. Ibid.
7. Charles Castle, *Noël* (Book Club Associates and W. H. Allen, 1973).
8. C. Murphy and J. Bryan, *The Windsor Story* (Granada Press, 1979).
9. Keith Middlemas, *Life and Times of George VI* (Weidenfeld and Nicolson, 1974).
10. Janet Flanner, *London was Yesterday* (Michael Joseph, 1975).
11. Ibid.

5

THE MONARCH AND
HIS MINSTRELS GO TO WAR

With the abrupt closing of theatres at the outbreak of war all but a handful of actors, actresses, variety artistes and circus performers found themselves redundant, but it soon became apparent that they would be needed to carry entertainment out of London to remote corners of this island and also to places abroad. There were small and large garrisons of troops, airmen and sailors who needed entertaining, if for no other reason than to take their minds off what was to come. This was where ENSA (Entertainment National Service Association or, as comedian Tommy Trinder later called it, 'Every Night Something Awful') came in. In the space of 24 hours a headquarters was established by the two people who were to be responsible for the running of the organisation, Sir Seymour Hicks and Basil Dean. The Theatre Royal Drury Lane became its base. This magnificent theatre, which went back hundreds of years, had closed in September 1939, when it was presenting yet another Ivor Novello success, *The Dancing Years*. This show, perhaps Novello's most successful, eventually went on tour and came back into the West End at the Adelphi Theatre, running in all for five years, a lot of it during the bombing of London by V1 and V2 guided missiles.

With the beginning of ENSA every available space in the famous theatre was taken over for rehearsals, administration offices, wardrobe and scenery store, etc. Artistes from all branches of entertainment, star names and unknowns, reported to Drury Lane to see if they could help. Whole productions were put together, small units mustered, or perhaps a solo artiste sent to an out-of-the-way anti-aircraft unit to entertain just a handful of men. Coaches could be seen leaving the theatre in the early hours of the morning with their charges, some of them to be taken to a port bound for an unknown destination overseas. Very early in its conception George VI and Queen Elizabeth came to visit ENSA at 'The Lane'. Their majesties talked with many of the artistes who were rehearsing, discussed the work of the wardrobe and scenery departments, and listened to the administrators giving instructions to the production managers. Ralph Reader of Boy Scout Gang Show fame had quickly been enlisted to get together a Service Gang Show to go to France. British security chiefs had assigned him, under cover of the show, to find the source of propaganda material that had been infiltrating some army units in France. Reader went on to produce many shows that later toured the Middle and Far East throughout the war, and his activities were certainly some of the most adventurous in the life of ENSA. He was justifiably awarded the CBE for his services, and his book *Ralph Reader Remembers* is compelling reading. ENSA eventually had its own comedy and music weekly radio programme, *ENSA Half Hour*.

George VI took his fair share of responsibility in the early months of the war. He was in constant touch with other heads of state and, perhaps more than any other monarch before him, was aware of both the international and domestic situations. He was loyal to Neville Chamberlain, although he knew there were many in the early 1940s who wanted the Prime Minister replaced. When Winston Churchill became head of government in May of that year, the King was impressed by his determination, and they had many informal meetings discussing the grave situation in Europe. The King never forgot that Neville Chamberlain had done his best, and remained his friend, visiting him when he was a dying man. It was His Majesty's humanity and sincerity that people of all walks of life admired about him, and later on his courage was to bring a respect few monarchs had experienced.

A state of war has always proved a godsend to song writers, and this war was no exception. A rabbit killed by a lone Nazi aeroplane in the Shetlands gave us 'Run Rabbit Run', made popular by Flanagan and Allen. 'We're Gonna Hang Out the Washing on the Siegfried Line' was another, prompted by the Nazi fortifications facing the French Maginot Line. By the early summer of 1940 this comic song wasn't so funny. 'Roll out the Barrel' had various versions, some of them vulgar in content. Noël Coward made his own inimitable contribution to the times with 'Don't Let's Be Beastly to the Germans', 'The Last Time I Saw Paris' and 'London Pride'. The latter was based on a traditional song, 'Won't you Buy my Sweet Blooming Lavender?' As Coward himself observed, 'This age old melody was appropriated by the Germans and used as a foundation for "Deutschland über Alles", and I considered that the time had come for us to have it back in London where it belonged.' 'We'll Meet Again', 'A Nightingale Sang in Berkeley Square', sung by Judy Campbell in 'New Faces' at the Comedy Theatre, 'Room Five Hundred and Four' and 'The White Cliffs of Dover' are just a few of the many wartime songs that have become standard 'pop'. Many musicians had joined the services and formed dance bands that were, because of the ingredients, first-class outfits. The Squadronaires, the Skyrockets and the Blue Mariners were all immensely popular. Some civilian bands like Joe Loss, Lew Stone, Geraldo and Jack Jackson came back into business at quite an early stage of hostilities; indeed, some of them had never ceased to operate.

The long winter nights seemed even longer with the total black-out which everyone conscientiously adhered to, but even that brought out the humour of the nation that was going to stand us in good stead in the future. An anecdote involving an air raid warden in the black-out was told and re-told in pubs and factories at the time. 'The warden on duty, seeing a shaft of light coming from a bedroom window, called out, "Hey, there's a chink in the room up there!" The reply from the lady of the house was "He's not a chink, he's a Japanese gentleman." ' Another story concerning the ARP involved the warden knocking on a door during an air raid and telling the occupant to get down in the shelter. An elderly voice from inside the house answered, 'I'll be out in a moment, I'm just going upstairs to get my teeth.' The warden shouted back, 'They're dropping bombs, not bloody sandwiches!' A charlady on a bus in the early morning said to her friend, 'There's this to be said for the bombing, it does take your mind off the black-out.' A nation has to survive when it has this sort of humour in its veins.

The BBC was the voice of the nation; the nine o'clock news was as popular as any programme, and the newsreaders became our friends with their calm relaying of events which were sometimes very alarming. The calm of Alvar Liddell, Bruce Belfrage and others must have been sorely tested at times in their small studios at Broadcasting House. At one period Broadcasting House itself was in danger when a 500-pound bomb exploded in the rear of the building, killing seven members of the staff, but still the evening news went ahead as usual. On another occasion an airborne mine landed in Portland Place, starting fires which raged for hours. Broadcasting House was deluged with water, but the staff technicians somehow kept the BBC on the air. An armoured car was stationed outside Broadcasting House during the war ready to drive the duty newsreaders to an auxiliary studio at Maida Vale if the building had been put out of action, but it was never required. The BBC Overseas Service from Bush House was terribly important for Allied friends in Europe and elsewhere. Radio created many wartime personalities: there was Tommy Handley, and later Jack Warner in *Garrison Theatre* and Bebe Daniels, Ben Lyon and Vic Oliver in *Hi Gang*. Household hints were brought to us *On The Home Front* and the *Radio Doctor* (Charles Hill, later to become Chairman of the Board of Governors of the BBC *and* Chairman of the Independent Television Authority) advised us on general health problems. Hill's manner was matey and warm, and I remember his fruity voice talking about the spread of germs and saying, 'Don't forget to wash your hands after you've been to the lavatory.' It was pretty daring at that time to use the word 'lavatory' in public. Wilfred Pickles was another broadcaster who became a household name, and of course later on presented his very popular *Have a Go* programme with 'Mabel [his wife] at the Table'. Organist Sandy Macpherson was a regular and highly respected broadcaster, and Vera Lynn, the Forces Sweetheart, is still happily entertaining us in her unique style. Programmes such as *Workers' Playtime, Music While You Work* and *Works Wonders* were all aimed at keeping up morale in the factories, but who would have thought that an intellectual half-hour called *The Brains Trust* could be such a huge success? The personalities in the programme really were extraordinary — Professor C. E. M. Joad with his catch-phrase 'Well, it all depends on what you mean by. . .', Commander Campbell, ex-navy, Harry Price the well known ghost hunter, and Julian Huxley. I met both Joad and Price, and they really were personalities. The man who made radio work for him in the most impressive way was Winston Churchill, and in turn, had it not been for radio I doubt whether his famous speeches would have had the impact on the nation that they did.

King George had sent his daughters up to Balmoral for a time until he had a better idea of how the war would be fought, but he and the Queen refused to leave London, even though there was little protection for them should the air raids start in any great quantity. Buckingham Palace didn't even have a proper air raid shelter. When the retreat in France and Belgium became unstoppable and Dunkirk was the only means of escape from Europe, something like 335,000 soldiers, most of them British, were safely evacuated. The King's position as far as he was concerned became quite clear now. He knew that he would be needed to visit the injured in rehabilitation centres all over the country, and that civilians needed to see their King amongst them. The threat of invasion was acute for a long time and if the monarch and his Queen had fled it would, in my opinion, have been one of the major disasters of the war. The fact that we knew they were staying here gave us a sense of confidence that we were going to survive. The Home Guard came into being in 1940; I remember my uncle answering Anthony Eden's nation-wide call almost before the Foreign Secretary had finished speaking. Uncle had been a captain in the First World War and had certainly been a courageous soldier, so when he joined the Home Guard he was made the local platoon captain. He came back after signing on and proceeded to take out, single-handed, practically all the furniture in the house and put it across the road, saying, 'That lot will hold them up until we can get reinforcements.' This was apparently just a rehearsal in case it was needed, because he immediately brought everything back into the house. It just goes to show that some of the situations in the television series *Dad's Army* were not as far-fetched as some viewers may have thought.

The establishment of the real Home Guard presented one comedian with an extension to his catch-phrase. Robb Wilton had, since 1939, begun his radio broadcasts with 'The Day War Broke Out. . .' Later he did a very funny routine which began:

> The day I joined the Home Guard, my missus said to me, 'What are you supposed to be?' I said, 'I'm one of the Home Guard.' She said, 'You?' I said, 'Yes,' she said, 'What do you do?' I said, 'I've got to stop Hitler's army from landing.' She said, 'What, just you?' I said, 'Of course not. There's Harry Bates, Charlie Evans, oh there's seven or eight of us altogether.'

Wilton's timing was superb, and the various characters he created were all based on a hesitant being who has to hide his fallibility under an umbrella of misplaced confidence. His Mr Muddlecombe JP was a masterpiece, and his off-stage humour is still talked about today. For instance, he was a great friend of Harry Tate, and he used to send Tate a postcard almost every week with the same message, 'Just off to Southampton', wherever he was going to or coming from. Another story about Robb Wilton comes from my old friend Algy More. Halfway through Robb's act at the Floral Hall in Harrogate an outdoor firework display began, and after a succession of very loud bangs Wilton paused and said to the audience, 'They're training me to be a police horse.' He was without doubt one of this country's great humorists.

Although theatre visits by the Royal Family were curtailed during the early period of the war, Queen Elizabeth did make the occasional outing, and her gesture in bringing her own food from the Palace was just another example of her thoughtfulness. There was strict rationing at that time, and Her Majesty knew that the staff at the theatre would try to obtain a little something special for her which would obviously be difficult in the circumstances. The Queen would have her meal in an ante-room in the interval. Another Queen, Victoria, was also in the habit of taking her own food to the theatre, but in contrast to Queen Elizabeth, Victoria could not wait for the interval and used to have her meal in the Royal Box while watching the performance.

As the country moved into the crucial Battle of Britain and then the blitz on London itself, the two princesses came back to Windsor Castle. Several pantomimes were produced at Windsor, with Princess Elizabeth and Princess Margaret playing principal roles, along with children of

Princess Margaret and Princess Elizabeth in a Windsor Castle production of *Cinderella*, December 1941. *Photograph courtesy of Theatre Museum*

Princess Elizabeth in the Windsor Castle production of *Old Mother Red Riding Boots*, December 1944. This was one of George VI's favourite photographs of the princess. *Photograph courtesy of Theatre Museum*

employees at the Castle. A headmaster from a school in Windsor was in charge of production, and Queen Elizabeth supervised the costuming. Both she and King George were very proud of their daughters in these productions.

George VI organised celebrity concerts at Windsor Castle, and his guests often included men and women from the services. One of the first of these concerts included the ukelele virtuoso George Formby. George was absolutely delighted with the invitation, but was a little worried that his songs in their usual form would not be acceptable to the Royal Family. The BBC had banned the broadcasting of some of his records, saying that they were too saucy, which must have hurt Formby, considering he was selling more records than practically anyone else at that time. Although his songs were only mildly *risqué*, he decided to alter some of the lyrics before going to Windsor Castle.

> When George and his wife Beryl arrived at Windsor an official of the King's household said, 'By the way, their majesties have especially asked that you give exactly the same show as you would to the troops — now don't forget.' Of course Formby was taken aback at this remark but heeded the 'Command'. The Royal family laughed as heartily as the troops when he sang the original version of 'Cleaning Windows'.[1]
> A night club Queen she looked divine, the Bridegroom he was doing fine, I'd rather have his job than mine, when I'm cleaning windows.[2]

After the concert George and Beryl were presented to the Royal Family, and he had obviously delighted them. Sone time later he was invited by Queen Mary to appear at Marlborough House when Her Majesty was entertaining servicemen. Before the concert the Queen said to George, 'I want to hear the same songs that you sang to my children.' It does seem strange on reflection that some of his songs, particularly 'Cleaning Windows', should have been frowned on by the BBC when they were so popular with the public, including the Royal Family. In fact the BBC apologised one night during the nine o'clock news for some disparaging remarks that had been made about Formby's song.

In 1941 George VI commanded George Black to bring the entire production of *Black Vanities* to Windsor Castle. *Vanities* was then running in London, starring Bud Flanagan and Chesney Allen. The whole company, including the stage staff and call boy, were taken to Windsor for the matinée performance. Before the show they were given a buffet meal, and changing accommodation was made available in the room where the Knights of the Garter were usually installed. On the way back from the buffet to the dressing-room one of the artistes saw a valet looking through the keyhole of another room. The valet told him that he had to wait there until their majesties had finished their lunch. The artiste, after looking through the keyhole himself, suggested to Chesney Allen that he might like to have a look, so Allen peeped through the keyhole and saw their majesties finishing their meal. After the show, when the cast was presented to the King and Queen, Bud Flanagan mentioned the keyhole incident to the King. His Majesty laughed and said, 'I wish I'd known, I keep a hat-pin for keyhole peepers.' King George had obviously enjoyed the show and chatted to Flanagan about his visits to the Palladium with the Queen when they were Duke and Duchess of York, and what fun they thought the shows had been.

Firth Shepherd's *Up and Doing* was another London production which was invited to Windsor Castle round about that time. Tommy Trinder's quick-fire wit had endeared himself not only to the theatre-going public but also to the service audiences to which he played on many occasions. The first time Trinder appeared before the King as King he reminded His Majesty that he had appeared before him when he was Duke of York. The King said, 'Yes, I remember. You've reached great heights since those days haven't you?' Trinder, who is unable to resist the quick retort, said, 'And you haven't done so badly yourself, Sir.' The comedian realised immediately that he might have gone too far, and hoped His Majesty hadn't taken offence. The King hadn't, and laughed about the incident when he repeated the joke to his family. On another occasion Trinder was entertaining in a concert on the lawns of Windsor Castle in the presence of George VI and every time he came to the tag of a gag it was drowned by low-flying RAF planes. Trinder, exasperated, turned to the King and said, 'Can't you do anything about them, Sir, after all you're the governor.' Several years later Tommy Trinder was entertaining in an after-dinner cabaret in the City, where Princess Margaret was one of the principal guests. Talking with him after the dinner, the Princess said to Tommy, 'My Papa loved you.' Trinder is very proud of the cuff-links decorated with the royal crest which George VI gave to him during his reign.

The King took his family to see some service shows in London during the war and showed his enjoyment of them. The American production of *This is the Army* included many well known hit songs, and their majesties joined in the choruses of such Irving Berlin classics as 'Alexander's Rag Time Band' and 'White Christmas'. The Canadian Senior Service also presented their own production, *Meet the Navy*, in the capital, and again the King was as enthusiastic as the rest of the audience. It is general knowledge that His Majesty liked to celebrate special family occasions with a visit to the theatre. For instance, on Princess Elizabeth's eighteenth birthday he took the Royal Family to the Palace Theatre to see *Something in the Air*, starring Jack Hulbert and Cicely Courtneidge. I remember seeing this show myself and thought it a superb evening's entertainment. The catchy title song kept you whistling and singing it long after first hearing the melody. Jack and Cicely were marvellous on stage, investing the whole production with their tremendous vitality and energy. They really were stars.

I, the Lord Chamberlain of The King's Household for the time being, do by virtue of my Office and in pursuance of powers given to me by the Act of Parliament for regulating Theatres, 6 & 7 Victoria, Cap 68, Section 12. Allow the Performance of a new Stage Play, of which a copy has been submitted to me by you, being a

play in 1 Act entitled

"Going Round The World"

with the exception of all Words and Passages which are specified in the endorsement of this Licence and without any further variations whatsoever.

Given under my hand this 16th day of September 1941.

Clarendon

Lord Chamberlain.

To The Manager of the Stolls Theatre.
Kingsway. W.2.

T 36

Until 1968 even a music hall sketch, classified as a one-act play, had to receive the Lord Chamberlain's seal of approval. Harry Tate's 'Going Round the World' was one such piece. *By courtesy of Ronnie Tate*

Nineteen forty-four will of course be best remembered for the opening of the Second Front. I was working in a factory at Southend, making spare parts for Spitfires and Hurricanes, and I clearly remember the morning of 6 June. We had heard on the factory radio that there was to be a special announcement, and when it came John Snagg's voice told us loud and clear that Allied troops had landed on the Normandy beaches. As Churchill had prophesied, we were back on French soil. If we had some misguided notion that it would now all be over in a couple of weeks, we were wrong. The Second Front brought its terrible toll of casualties; Arnhem was just one instance. In this country a sinister new menace appeared in the skies with the coming of Hitler's secret weapons, the V1 and V2. They caused terrible casualties in the last year of the war. I remember being on a train travelling from Southend to Fenchurch Street and seeing a doodlebug (V1) practically following alongside the train before suddenly making its dive on to an unsuspecting and indiscriminate target.

Within a few days of the Second Front opening King George landed in France, where he talked to soldiers on the beach-head, and decorated some of them for gallantry in the field. Shortly afterwards he went to Italy to see the British troops there who had already endured fierce fighting and felt somewhat forgotten in view of the publicity the French landings had received. General Alexander was delighted and grateful to the King for this urgently needed morale booster. His Majesty was also in Paris and Brussels immediately after the two capitals were liberated.

In December 1944 one of the world's great band leaders disappeared on a flight from London to Paris and was never heard of again. Glen Miller, whose music so epitomised the wartime years, was lost, but his music has stayed with us and is still popular today.

On 8 May 1945 the war in Europe was over. I will certainly never forget that night. Along with two friends I went up to London and walking, or rather pushing, my way through Trafalgar Square I sensed that people were slightly dazed rather than jubilant. We all knew that now we could take down the black-out screens, that we needn't follow the 'White Line' any more, that we could sleep an uninterrupted sleep, that we didn't have to 'Dig for Victory' any longer, but perhaps it was all too much to take in so soon. As we edged our way nearer to Buckingham Palace the atmosphere became bawdier, people were trying to dance with one another, and couples were kissing on any available space in St James's Park, interrupted only by the noise of the ducks and moorhens on the lake who must have wondered what all the fuss was about. One of my friends made the acquaintance of a member of the WAAF (Women's Auxiliary Air Force) and disappeared into the night.

He and I didn't meet up again until a fortnight later, when he told me he was going to marry his VE night WAAF. He did and they eventually took a pub in Berkshire, but he was killed in a car crash shortly afterwards.

I eventually made my way on Victory Night to a point half-way up the Mall. It was impossible to get any closer to the Palace, but you knew even from that distance that their majesties were making regular appearances on the balcony — the applause and cheering from the crowd told you. Little did I know that just ahead of me two rather special young ladies were joining in the celebrations. The King had given Princess Elizabeth and Princess Margaret permission to join the crowd in the Mall.

King George must have been so thankful, as we all were, that at least part of the war was over. I'm sure he was tired of the responsibility he had shared with the nation during its five years of anxiety. Personal tragedy had befallen him in 1942 when his brother, the Duke of Kent, was killed in a flying accident. I know how he must have felt. My own brother died in similar circumstances in 1941.

We had all been singing a popular song of the day, 'I'm Going to Get Lit Up when the Lights Go Up in London', several weeks before they finally did. Noël Coward was not slow to light up the London theatrical scene in 1945. His new revue *Sigh No More*, starring Graham Payn and Joyce Grenfell, was full of the witty Coward, and contained a particularly haunting song called 'Matelot', one of my favourite show melodies. Noël Coward hadn't been idle during the war years. He spent many months entertaining service personnel at home and abroad, and had also been responsible for the production of a marvellous film about the navy, *In Which We Serve*. It was based on the story of Lord Mountbatten's famous little ship, HMS *Kelly*. Coward not only wrote and produced the film, he co-directed it with David Lean and starred in it as the captain of the doomed vessel. *In Which We Serve* won a special Academy Award. The man's talent was unbelievable.

The Victory Royal Variety Performance on 5 November at the London Coliseum included Webster Booth and Anne Ziegler, who were making an enormous reputation with their singing of romantic ballads. They were later copied by many duettists in the concert world, but never bettered. They recently returned to this country from a long stay overseas and were enthusiastically welcomed home by a legion of fans who remembered their hey-day with affection. Wilson, Kepple and Betty repeated their sand dance routine, and Vic Oliver, the American comedian who had made his name along with Bebe Daniels and Ben Lyon in the wartime radio show *Hi Gang*, was in fine form. Tommy

Trinder was there, assisted by band leader Chappie D'Amato. Will Hay, with his company, was making his fourth Royal Variety appearance. One of Hay's assistants in his scholastic comedy routines was Peter Byrne, who featured as Sgt. Andy Crawford in the long-running TV series *Dixon of Dock Green*. Duggie Wakefield and company were back again in this show. Also appearing was comedian George Doonan, singing star Delya, and Sid Field and Jerry Desmonde, who were making their royal début. Field had come into London from the provinces in 1943 and taken the capital by storm, but more about him later. A big success in this production was the appearance of the amazing Colleano family, Maurice, George and Bonar. They had a circus background as entertainers, and Bonar went on to further stardom on stage and in films. A complete extrovert, he was a great character in the post-war entertainment scene. An unfortunate car accident while he was appearing in Liverpool robbed the theatre of a very talented performer. This Royal Performance, the first since 1938, had been a great success and in the ensuing years we were to see a boom in the theatre, not only in London but all over the country.

Notes

1. Alan Randall and Ray Seaton, *George Formby* (W. H. Allen, 1974).
2. Part lyrics from song, ibid.

6
'WHAT A PERFORMANCE!'

The post-war theatre in this country really had a captive audience just waiting to be entertained. With the right productions, reputations of performers, writers and impresarios could be made overnight. On 7 June 1946 television in this country restarted from Alexandra Palace, but it was still in its infancy. Radio was listened to by millions and it was the personalities who were heard in 'sound' only that the public wanted to see in the theatre. Live shows and the cinema were the popular entertainment venues whether it was in the large cities or outside. Even what show business called the No. 3s and No. 2s were doing well. They were the smaller provincial halls, somewhat draughty and damp back-stage and front of house, like the Palace Attercliffe, the Empire Portsmouth, the Hippodrome Aldershot and, probably the best known of all, Collins Music Hall at Islington in north London. People like Charlie Chaplin and Norman Wisdom played there in their early days.

One story about Collins and its famous owner Lew Lake was told by a comedian who came into the bar after the first house on Monday and said to Lew Lake, who was having his usual Monday night drink, 'Not a very good house tonight, Lew,' to which Lake replied, 'Well, what can you expect, with Polo at Hurlingham?' All theatre managers had an excuse for bad business, but this reply must have been the most outrageous — I doubt if anyone in Islington had ever heard of Hurlingham, let alone polo.

Even if these theatres left something to be desired, they were open fifty-two weeks a year presenting variety, touring revue and pantomime, and consequently gave employment to many artistes, a lot of whom in 1946 had returned from service abroad entertaining the troops. For those starting out in the profession the No. 3s and 2s were a marvellous training ground. There is nowhere similar today to obtain the grounding they could provide. Repertory theatres in a more sophisticated form are still there for the straight actor, but the provincial variety theatre is really no more.

In London in 1946 the Hippodrome Theatre was still having a huge success with Ivor Novello's *Perchance to Dream*. The Theatre Royal

Comedian Sid Field and his 'tutor' Jerry Desmonde in 'Golfing', included in the first post-war Royal Variety Performance in 1945. *Photograph courtesy of BBC Hulton Picture Library*

Drury Lane was presenting a not too successful Noël Coward musical, *Pacific 1860*, starring Mary Martin, which incidentally George VI saw during its comparatively short run at the 'Lane'. The London Palladium was staging the revue *High Time*, starring Jimmy Jewel and Ben Warris, and the musical *The Song of Norway* was at the Palace Theatre. The Prince of Wales Theatre in Coventry Street was featuring a revue called *Piccadilly Hayride*, starring Sid Field.

It had been just three short years since Field had come into London unknown, and almost overnight had become a star. The word 'star' is so very often abused, but Sid Field was one in every sense of the word. This Birmingham-born comedian had been touring the provinces for many years, and George Black brought him to the West End in a revue called *Strike a New Note*. Everyone in this show was an unknown artiste, but the cast included Eric Morecambe, Ernie Wise (not working as a double act then), Sheila Mathews, Derek Roy and Zoe Gail. All of them went on to achieve fame over the years, but it was Sid Field whose name went down in theatrical history at the Prince of Wales. A few days after the opening of *Strike a New Note* George Black put Sid's name up in lights outside the theatre, and well he deserved it. In 1946 Field appeared in his second Royal Variety Performance and also a Royal Film Performance. His royal début was in 1945 in the presence of the King and Queen and their two daughters. This was the first time Princess Elizabeth and Princess Margaret had attended a Royal Variety Performance, and in fact it was their first visit to a variety show. In that royal show in 1945 Sid Field, along with his superb feed Jerry Desmonde, performed their very funny golfing sketch which had been featured in *Strike a New Note* and the sequel, *Strike it Again*. In this sketch Field enters wearing a large sweater, loud golfing trousers, cap and an assortment of golf clubs. Desmonde, in smart attire, is the Pro-teacher, and Sid the Rabbit:

Desmonde:	Right, now first of all make the 'tee'.
Field:	Make the 'tea', I thought we were going to play golf.
Desmonde:	Make the 'tee' of sand.
Field:	'Tea' of sand? Don't be so foolhardy, I'm not drinking that stuff — 'tea' of sand, be more like Cocoa.
Desmonde:	All right, skip it. (Field jumps over ball.) What are you jumping over the ball for?
Field:	Well, you just said skip it.
Desmonde:	(getting cross with Field) No, no, now come on, get behind the ball.
Field:	(starting to shout) It's behind all the way round. What a performance.

And so it went on. It is difficult to describe the real essence of Sid Field's comedy, but it certainly was a performance. He had tremendous charm, a great rapport with the audience, and of course he was a really funny man. His comedy had a tinge of 'camp' about it, but at that time 'camp' wasn't really understood. When Desmonde got annoyed and impatient with him, Field would fly into a mock temper. After some silly rantings and sometimes grotesque contortions around the motionless figure of his feed, Field would stop abruptly and give the audience a sly smile.

Desmonde, feeling he might have gone too far with Field, would put his arm round the comedian and try it all again with quiet persuasion, which of course made no difference to Sid's confused reaction.

In the 1946 Royal Variety Show, Sid Field played his 'Billiards' sketch, assisted by Jerry Desmonde and Alfie Dean. Field's pocketing of the ball routine in this piece was comedy at its best. When told to pocket the ball he looked baffled for a moment, then, with a smile, put the ball in his trouser pocket and started to walk away with a ridiculous grin on his face, as if to say, 'I don't know who's more stupid, them or me.' His 'Slasher Green' character, 'The Photographer' and other comedy creations were masterpieces.

Terry Thomas, who was appearing in *Piccadilly Hayride* at the time, was included in this royal show. Not many people know that Terry Thomas started his career as a film extra and went on to appear in cabaret and variety as an impressionist. His act consisted of appearing as a BBC radio disc jockey, complete with turntable (that was a DJ's image 35 years ago). In a very upper-class voice Thomas would say, 'How-do-you-do' (it became a catch-phrase in its way), 'tonight I'd like to play some of your requests. . .' At this point he would realise that the records were missing, and so would start his rather eccentric and absurd impressions of the artistes we should have heard on record. A very funny piece both vocally and visually. Terry Thomas eventually went on to make a big name for himself in films, both here and in Hollywood. He always had great style.

Making the first of what would be many royal appearances were Jimmy Jewell and Ben Warris, a comedy double act that exploited Jewell's stage stupidity to the full. His cousin Warris was a magnificent feed in their long partnership. They dissolved their stage partnership at the end of the sixties and went their separate ways, but happily both are still making us laugh. Also making their royal début were Nat Mills and Bobby. This top-of-the-bill husband and wife duo were very funny and played seasons at the big resorts and on tour with their own show. Their catch-phrase, 'Let's get on with it,' was familiar to millions of radio listeners. The Musical Director for the whole production was Paul Fenoulet, with the Skyrockets Orchestra. I got to know Paul very well when he was in charge of the BBC Variety Orchestra for programmes such as *Midday Music Hall, Saturday Night Variety* and *Beyond our Ken*. He was an extremely kind and helpful man and always a joy to work with.

George VI liked informal visits to the theatre rather more than official occasions. Of course he knew that these visits to the theatre were nearly always presented for the purpose of raising money for charity, and being the responsible and sensitive man he was, he was always happy to attend.

About this time the King and his family paid an informal visit to the Strand Theatre to see Firth Shephard's farce, *Fifty-Fifty*. The theatre management did not have a box available for the royal party at this performance and instead offered them seats in the dress circle. The King's reaction was, 'Well, we shall have a good view tonight.' Most theatre boxes, although there are exceptions, are angled to cut off the view of at least a part of the stage, so one can understand the King's remark.

A meeting between Bud Flanagan and Jack Hylton towards the end of 1946 was to have a significant effect on the fortunes of the Victoria Palace Theatre and the careers of the Crazy Gang for some time to come. Hylton and Flanagan both decided that it was time that they all did another show together. Chesney Allen, who had been Bud Flanagan's partner for a long time, decided he would retire from actively working with the Gang, but would stay on as their business manager, and so it was Allen together with Hylton who planned the new show. It was called *Together Again* and opened at the Victoria Palace in March 1947. It was very soon apparent that George VI was happy at the reunion because he was a great fan of the Gang. He took Queen Elizabeth to a performance of the show on Her Majesty's birthday, and at the start of the show the Gang all sang 'Happy Birthday', with the audience joining in. In the interval Bud Flanagan and the 'boys' were invited to meet their majesties in the manager's office, where the Queen thanked them for their birthday greetings and said to Bud, 'You know, the Victoria Palace is my local' (it is just across the road from Buckingham Palace). Princess Margaret had already seen the show and the King said, 'Is this the show my daughter Princess Margaret saw?' Bud said, 'Yes, Sir, with a few exceptions, we cut out a gag or two.' The King smiled and said, 'You put them all back again in the second half.' The Gang did, and a few more besides.

I suppose 'The Yanks are Coming' could have been the theatrical theme song for this period in the forties. Two American musicals took London by storm in 1947; *Oklahoma*, starring Howard (then Harold) Keel, made a tremendous impact when it opened at the Theatre Royal Drury Lane. It was full of vitality and energy, and nothing quite like it had been seen on the London stage before. It was an overwhelming success for its creators, Richard Rodgers and Oscar Hammerstein II, and ran for a total of 1,548 performances in London. It has recently been revived in the West End at the Palace Theatre, again playing to packed houses, and directed by Oscar Hammerstein's son. The Irving Berlin musical *Annie Get Your Gun* had its London opening in the same year, and ran for only a little less time than *Oklahoma*, over 1,300 performances. This show starred Americans Dolores Gray and Bill

Johnson, and also Irving Davies, who has gone on to choreograph many stage and television productions in this country. Of course the Americans didn't have it all their own way in the theatre. At the Adelphi Theatre the very successful Vivian Ellis and A. P. Herbert musical *Bless the Bride* was running, presented by the great C. B. Cochrane, directed and choreographed by Wendy Toye, and starring Lizbeth Webb, George Guetary, Brian Reece and Betty Paul. King George saw both *Annie Get Your Gun* and *Bless the Bride*: in fact he saw *Annie* twice.

Two of the funniest men in the world arrived in this country from America in 1947, one an Englishman, Stan Laurel, and his partner, Oliver Hardy. They were popular then, as a result of their many Hollywood films over the years, but they have now become a cult through the showing on television of a great many of their early 'shorts'. Laurel and Hardy appeared in the 1947 Royal Variety Performance at the Palladium, with a specially written piece of material. Laurel was quite at home on the stage, as his career had started in the theatre with Fred Karno's company in England. Laurel, born Jefferson, was the son of actor/manager/playwright A. J. Jefferson, who for several years ran the old Metropole Theatre in Glasgow. Jefferson Junior went to America with Karno in company with Charlie Chaplin and, like Chaplin, stayed there. He changed his surname to Laurel and, again like Chaplin, was engaged by the pioneering film-makers. Being a pantomimist, the silent movies suited Stan's inventive comedy, and by the mid-twenties he was engaged by the Hal Roach studios in Hollywood. It was here that he met another contract artiste, Oliver Norvell Hardy, ex-boy soprano, kindly and fat, who had already been involved in theatre management. In his early films as an actor of some merit Hardy always portrayed the villain, but of course it was his teaming with Stan Laurel that was the stroke of genius on the part of the studio and Stan Laurel. If Stan was the creative comedy mind behind their partnership it was the jolly Oliver Hardy who made the most of it. His long looks to the camera when Laurel had got them into 'another fine mess' were a new innovation as far as film-making was concerned and the technique is still used today by comedy entertainers in television. Visually Laurel and Hardy will never be bettered, and if copying is the greatest form of flattery, then the 'boys' have been flattered to a degree unknown before in show business. They made a limited variety tour in this country and were received with enormous warmth and affection wherever they went.

Also appearing with Stan and Ollie in the 1947 royal show was Bobbie Kimber, a female impersonator ventriloquist (unusual to say the least) and American Jack Durant, a large man who did a very funny routine impersonating Sidney Greenstreet and Peter Lorre. I saw Durant at the

Stan Laurel and Oliver Hardy, in this country for their appearance in the 1947 Royal Variety Performance, took time off to reopen the Romney Hythe and Dymchurch Railway. *Photograph courtesy of BBC Hulton Picture Library*

Palladium, and for the 'Greenstreet' bit he would shove a cushion up his jacket, say a couple of words, then return to his 'Peter Lorre', saying only another couple of words. The whole routine was made extremely funny by the clipped short dialogue and long pauses in between. He was yet another performer who didn't rely on jokes.

Tommy Trinder was in this show and, with his wit and brilliant off-the-cuff humour, had already shown he was quite at home in the company of the Royal Family. Trinder and the Crazy Gang were often detailed to do the warm-up before the show actually started to relax the audience and break down any feeling of reserve in the theatre. The artistes who do the early spots in the royal performance sometimes get an indifferent reaction from the audience, which is not difficult to understand. They are paying a lot of money on these occasions, all of which of course goes to charity, but nevertheless the thought is 'Well, come on, entertain us.' A great majority of these people are regular West End theatre-goers and have seen it all before. They tend to laugh and

Tommy Trinder with Sidney Jerome at the piano entertaining in the village hall, Windsor Great Park, December 1947. *Below*: the audience includes Princess Margaret, George VI and Queen Elizabeth. *Photograph courtesy of BBC Hulton Picture Library*

applaud only when the royal party react. Before they enter the theatre the audience has generally had a hard time. Streets are choked with traffic in the vicinity and parking places are at a premium. Taxis are scarce, and when one is found it will take a long time to travel a short distance. So one can appreciate the mood of some of the paying customers when they do finally get to the theatre. Therefore the pre-show warm-up has become very important and has often been planned with the same detail as the performance itself. Tommy Trinder, doing a warm-up, told the audience what they had been like the year before, reminding them they had frightened the artistes by their indifference. He quoted the previous year's press criticism of themselves and said, 'If I'd had such lousy write-ups I wouldn't show my face in here again, but you're back, bold as brass.' Tommy obviously made his point because the audience laughed and from then on all went well. The Crazy Gang in an opening warm-up engaged in antics in the Royal Box, disguised as Palladium cleaning staff, tossing out old programmes, ice-cream cartons, etc. from the box. Bud Flanagan also rushed into the stalls, grabbed the Marquis of Blandford and hauled him out of his seat, ripping out his shirt front. It was in fact a paper dickie which he had earlier agreed to put on to help Bud with the gag. At one warm-up Flanagan told the audience he hoped they would enjoy the show and laugh when they really felt like it and not just when the Royal Family laughed, as the audience sometimes do. 'Don't keep looking at the Royal Box every time you hear a gag,' said Bud, 'you'll get on their bloody nerves.' That certainly broke the ice.

King George and Queen Elizabeth had their own production to organise in November of that year. Their daughter, Princess Elizabeth, was marrying her naval lieutenant Philip Mountbatten, the nephew of the respected Lord Louis. How the public loved the whole romantic atmosphere of the royal betrothal after the austere years of the forties. One must remember that pretty well everything was still rationed and in short supply; petrol in fact was banned for private use. Mother and father, who had endured the privations of these years with their subjects, were now able to enjoy their daughter's special day with the whole nation. Television brought views of the pageantry into millions of homes for the first time. It was about this time that the BBC began to experiment with new camera techniques, which were used for the first time when an episode of Tommy Handley's *ITMA* was televised in a studio at Broadcasting House in the presence of the King and Queen. As I have mentioned earlier, *ITMA* was regarded as George VI's favourite radio programme — in fact the King had a radio set in his bathroom so that he needn't miss an episode of the show should it happen to coincide with his bathtime.

Nineteen forty-eight seemed to herald a new feeling of optimism in the country. The King and Queen celebrated their Silver Wedding and the theatre was getting back on its feet in a big way, with the Royal Family frequent patrons. Perhaps one of the most sensational happenings on the London stage was the appearance of American Danny Kaye at the Palladium. Danny was the toast of the town, and the whole Royal Family went to see him on more than one occasion. During a performance one day Danny looked off-stage and said, 'I wouldn't half like a cup of tea.' A few minutes later a lady from the back-stage staff wandered on with a cuppa for a surprised Kaye, which got a big laugh from the audience. This little bit of business was kept in as a regular occurrence. When King George VI, accompanied by the Queen, Princess Elizabeth, Princess Margaret and the Duke of Edinburgh went to a performance they all sat in the front stalls. At a given point during Danny's act he asked for his cup of tea and a lady duly brought it on behind him. Danny then asked the audience what they were laughing at, and the King said in a loud voice, 'You've got a cup of tea.' You can imagine what a laugh that got. Princess Margaret and Princess Elizabeth both visited Kaye in his dressing-room, where he was delighted to see them. The first time Princess Elizabeth saw him back-stage she invited him to join her and the Duke of Edinburgh, and their party, to dinner. Kaye declined, saying he had another engagement. Actually the real reason was that he felt too nervous to accept. He was told afterwards by the management that it is not 'the done thing' to decline a royal invitation. I'm sure the Princess understood. Danny Kaye had made his name in films and on records, with songs like 'Ballin the Jack', 'Minnie the Moocher' and 'Little White Duck'. He made many friends when he was over here, amongst them Sid Field. They became great buddies and also admired one another's work. Kaye made a great fuss of Sid when he visited America, giving a luncheon in honour of the English comedian to which many Hollywood film stars were invited.

Danny also became very matey with our own Ted Ray, who was on the same bill as himself at the Palladium. Ray used to introduce Danny to the audience each night. Soap was still on ration at the time, and one night Danny had to borrow a piece from Ted. Ted asked him to let him have it back when he'd washed, as it was in short supply. When Danny got back to America he sent Ted a whole case. Unfortunately Danny Kaye wasn't a big success in the 1948 Royal Variety Performance at the Palladium, probably because he hadn't taken into account the sort of audience who come to see these shows. They are a little more sophisticated than the normal audience, and as most of them had probably seen Danny already during his season in London, I suspect they expected too much of him on the royal night. Ted Ray, however, was a huge success in this performance. His opening line was: 'I've been in this business forty years and now I'm down to doing a one-night stand.' I virtually started my radio career with Ted in *Ray's a Laugh*: he was a super bloke, with a sense of humour as sharp as a razor. I learned a lot from the great Ted Ray.

Danny Kaye had a chance towards the end of the show to finish on a high note when he joined Bud Flanagan and Chesney Allen in a chorus of their popular 'Underneath the Arches'. This was the show that introduced a very young Julie Andrews to the Royal Family. Julie had an exceptional voice even at that time, and she finished by standing on a chair leading the entire company in the National Anthem. It was certainly one of the great bills assembled for a Royal Variety Performance.

In the meantime great advances had been made in television. The Oxford and Cambridge Boat Race was followed for the first time by a portable camera on a following launch, so that the whole race was seen by viewers, who were treated to a thrilling finish, Cambridge winning by a quarter of a length. The first weather forecast was transmitted, though the weather was hardly worth transmitting in 1949. An anxious

Chesney Allen, Danny Kaye and Bud Flanagan during rehearsals for the 1948 Royal Variety Performance. *Photograph courtesy of BBC Hulton Picture Library*

time for everyone, particularly his family, was the period of George VI's illness. He had an operation early in the year which proved successful, and though his recovery took a long time, he did make progress and was able to resume his duties.

The theatre was still booming in the late forties. Princess Elizabeth and Princess Margaret went to see the very successful *Brigadoon* at His Majesty's Theatre, where one of the stars was Noele Gordon — star of *Crossroads*. King George, together with the Queen, Princess Margaret and the Crown Prince and Princess of Norway went to Wyndham's Theatre to see *Daphne Laureola*. The Prince of Wales Theatre was staging another Sid Field success, this time a straight play, *Harvey*. Sid was marvellous in it. I saw him in this production, and I also saw Joe E. Brown who took over the part of the central character, Elwood P. Dowd, when Sid had to leave the play for a rest. Princess Margaret saw *Harvey* early in 1949 and, probably on her recommendation, the King and Queen, Princess Elizabeth and the Duke of Edinburgh, together with Princess Margaret, went to see it later in the summer.

The Royal Variety Performance of that year was held at the Coliseum, and included for the first time in a royal show the magical Frenchman Maurice Chevalier. Topping the bill was the great Ted Ray, given this honour after his success the previous year.

In 1950 the Crazy Gang were packing them in at the Victoria Palace with their *Knights of Madness*, and a royal visit was made to the show by Princess Margaret accompanied by the Marquis of Blandford. The Dame Irene Vanburgh memorial matinée at the Theatre Royal Drury Lane was attended by the Queen, Princess Elizabeth and Princess Margaret. The Palladium continued with its policy of variety headed by big American stars which was established in 1947 with the successful appearance of entertainers like Laurel and Hardy, and, in 1948, Danny Kaye. Early in 1950 the theatre world was shocked by the death of Sid Field. I was absolutely shattered when I heard the news. He was only in his forties and had so much more to give to the business. Sid's enormous success in the West End had spanned such a short period that he hadn't been able to accumulate any real money, so a benefit concert was arranged at the Palladium to help his family. Everyone in the business wanted to be a part of that tribute to Sid. It was organised by the Palladium boss Val Parnell, Danny Kaye, Bud Flanagan and Bill Little, the owner of the Albany Club. The theatre staff gave their services free, and artistes came from far and wide for this performance to pay their tribute to a great performer: Laurence Olivier, Judy Garland, Orson Welles assisted in some magic by Elizabeth Taylor, Arthur Askey, Bud Flanagan, Tommy Trinder, Cicely Courtneidge, Douglas Fairbanks, Jack Buchanan,

Margaret Lockwood, Ted Ray, the dancers currently appearing at the Palladium, Victoria Palace and Prince of Wales theatres, and Danny Kaye trying to learn something about the art of cricket from sporting hero Denis Compton. Artistes took part in production numbers specially written for the show, and the evening was brought to a close with everyone singing, 'There's No Business Like Show Business'. There was a written tribute to Sid Field in the programme:

> Genius is supposed to be moody, difficult, hard to live with, but there was a genius — called Sid Field — who was none of these things. Sid was a comedian, a maker of laughter, a great clown whose inspiration came from an understanding of the hair's breadth which separates tears and laughter.

The 1950 Royal Variety Show at the London Palladium was staged in the presence of George VI, Queen Elizabeth, Princess Elizabeth and Princess Margaret; included in the performance were Billy Cotton and his band. Billy's son, Bill Cotton, is now Assistant Managing Director of BBC Television. Also appearing was Donald Peers, who was a big name through his radio shows and stage appearances. Peers' signature tune, 'Babbling Brook', was as well known to the public as the sound of the cuckoo. He was Britain's most popular crooner. Max Wall was making another appearance in a royal performance. Max, a legendary variety artiste, has now gone legitimate and has become as popular in this field as he was in his earlier career. As everybody knows, Max, as a variety artiste, had his lean years, but has bounced back in a big way. I worked in variety with him during those difficult times, and I remember a week at Sunderland we did together. The audience were not giving him much encouragement, but he plodded on twice nightly doing his own thing. I used to stand at the side of the stage and watch him regularly. One rainy morning he came with me to buy a pair of shoes, and when I had purchased them he asked the assistant if she had a pair like mine in size eleven. Now Max has very tiny feet and when the girl brought the elevens he said, 'I can't wear those, they'll fall off all over the High Street.' I think I am one of the world's worst gigglers, and I had to leave the shop helpless with laughter. In spite of the wet week, and some rather unfashionable digs, it was six days of fun with Max.

Frankie Howerd, who made his Royal Variety Performance début in the same year, wasn't pleased with his efforts, but then Frankie has always been self-critical. Max Bygraves bounced into his first royal show, as did the great American comedian Jack Benny. I saw him at the Palladium with some of the stars from his radio programmes. I remember Phil Harris, who had made a niche for himself with fast wordy songs like 'Woodman Spare that Tree' and 'Dark Town Poker Club', singer

1	Freddie Bretherton	9	Sam Brown	16	George Swift
2	Billy Ternent	10	Peter Yorke	17	Les Carew
3	Jack Hylton	11	Johnnie Raites	18	?
4	Sonny Farrar	12	Jack Jackson	19	Dick Willows
5	Bruce Trent	13	Chappie D'Amato	20	Paul Fenoulet
6	Eddie Hooper	14	'Poggie' Pogson	21	Eric Breeze
7	Freddie Schweitzer	15	Joe Crossman	22	Stanley Andrews
8	?				

Jack Hylton gathered together many of his original musicians and singers for the 1950 Royal Variety Performance. By 1950 most of them had become leaders in their own right. *Photograph courtesy of Bruce Trent*

Dennis Day, and Rochester, who was Benny's 'man Friday'. Phil Harris would tear the audience apart with a couple of songs, and on would walk Benny staring at the audience all the while Harris was taking his calls, which were several. Benny would look off into the wings, back again to the audience and when silence was almost complete after a further pause would say, in an off-hand way, 'I don't see it myself.' With Benny, it was the expectancy of what he was going to say, teed up by the long pauses, that brought the big laughs. You were watching a craftsman at work.

In a roundabout way it was Jack Benny who caused the back-stage drama in that 1950 royal show, although nothing to do with him personally. He had been allotted something like twenty minutes for his spot that night, not unreasonably as he had come over from America, where he was a legend. British comedian Max Miller was given six minutes for his act. Now Miller was a huge bill topper, and as famous as any of the music-hall greats: one well known columnist, Bill Boorne, called him 'The Pure Gold of the Music Hall'. On this occasion Max abandoned the routine he had rehearsed and added several different gags. The audience was enjoying all the Miller fire, but he was running well over his allotted time. One of the courtesies to the Royal Family is to try to get the show done on time — after all, it is as long an evening for them as it is for anyone else. As it became apparent that Max was going to run longer than he should, he was getting calls from producer Charles Henry on the side of the stage to 'Come off, Max.' Waiting behind the curtains were Jack Hylton and his musicians and singers from his earlier band days ready for their spot of nostalgia. Singer Bruce Trent was one of those waiting with Hylton, and he remembers the band leader calling Max to come off. When eventually Miller did, Val Parnell, 'The Guv'nor', was furious and said to him, 'You'll never work in one of my theatres [Moss Empires] again.' Max said, 'You're £25,000 too late.' This referred to the fact that he had already made his money during his long career playing the theatres. Inevitably, the newspapers got to hear about it, and there were headlines for several days. Opinions were divided. Some said Max was entitled to be angry at the short amount of time he had been given in comparison to Jack Benny, others that Val Parnell was the boss and Max should have abided by his decision. Bud Flanagan, who was also in the show, summed up the situation thus:

> Protocol must be observed, and everyone on and off the stage must respect it. Whatever some stars may think of themselves at a Royal show the top of the bill is the Monarch, and we the artistes have the privilege of performing in support.

The Royal Family were unaware of this little drama at the time, and thoroughly enjoyed the show.

We the undersigned, tender our Sincere Congratulations to Bud Flanagan (Flanagan & Allen) on being one of the Representative Artistes selected to appear at the Royal Command Variety Performance held at the London Palladium on Monday November 13th 1950. in the Presence of Their Majesties, The King and Queen. The Performance being in aid of the Variety Artistes Benevolent Fund and Institution for Indigent Variety and Circus Artistes.

Scroll presented to Bud Flanagan commemorating his appearance in the Royal Variety Performance, November 1950. *By courtesy of Grand Order of Water Rats*

Nineteen fifty-one was the year of the Festival of Britain. It was an occasion to demonstrate that Britain could fly the flag and 'put on a show'. Celebrations to mark the event took place all over the country, but it was London that visitors came to in great numbers to see what the 'old country' could do. The South Bank west of Waterloo Bridge was the site chosen for the building of the Festival Hall. The National

Portrait in oils of Bud Flanagan by Robert Lenkiewicz. *By courtesy of Grand Order of Water Rats. Photograph Doug McKenzie, PPS*

Theatre now stands on the east side of the bridge — the cause of some controversy when it was built, but doubtless due to take its place among our national monuments in the future. The Festival Gardens, with a fun fair, were on the South Bank at Battersea. The opening of the Festival in May was attended by the King and Queen, the princesses and other members of the Royal Family.

King George and Queen Elizabeth, accompanied by the princesses, saw *The Little Hut*, starring Robert Morley, at the Lyric Theatre, and attended a charity performance of *Gay's the Word* with Cicely Courtneidge at the Saville. Judy Garland was topping the bill at the Palladium. I was present on the opening night and witnessed her famous trip and subsequent fall on her bottom as she walked on to the accompaniment of her famous signature tune. The applause for that little bundle of energy was deafening. Princess Margaret went to the second house of the variety bill headed by Bob Hope then at the Prince of Wales

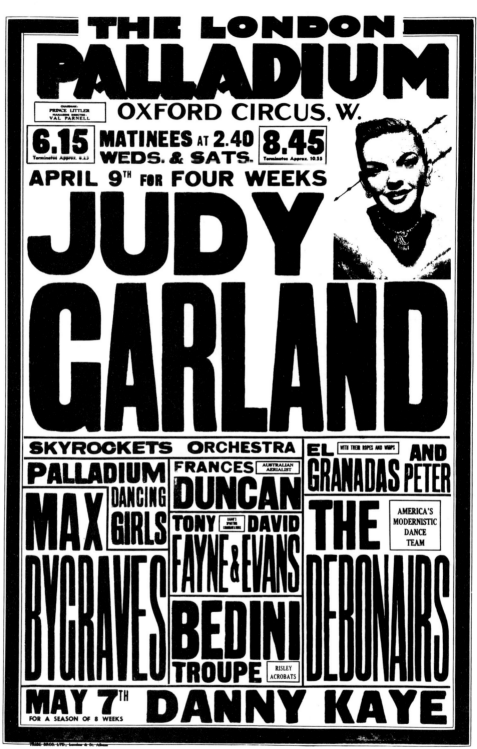

Palladium bill, 9 April 1951. *By courtesy of Moss Empires Ltd*

Theatre, and attended her first London *première* of a play, *Relative Values*, at the Savoy in November.

Again in 1951 there was anxiety about the King's health. He had a further operation in September, and after a slow period of convalescence was able to spend Christmas with his family at Sandringham. With a trip to South Africa in the offing, he was looking forward to getting back into harness. Ben Lyon, who was producing the stage presentation at a Royal Film Performance in November 1951, knew that the King, due to his illness, would not be able to attend the performance. A few days before the show was due to take place, Bebe, Ben's wife, thought it would be a nice idea to send His Majesty some flowers wishing him well. Ben wondered whether it would be right to do so but, and I can hear him saying it, said, 'You go ahead, honey, and send them,' which Bebe did. After the film performance on the night Ben and Bebe were presented to the Queen. She said to Ben, 'Mr Lyon, the flowers you and your wife sent to the King were beautiful.' Ben couldn't resist saying, 'Did His Majesty actually see them?' The Queen replied, 'Yes, they are in his room.'[1] Bebe Daniels and Ben Lyon were two American entertainers with a great loyalty to Britain and our Royal Family, whom they met more than once.

Because of the King's illness he was unable to attend the Royal Variety Performance at the Victoria Palace in October, but it was attended by Her Majesty the Queen, Princess Margaret, the Duchess of Gloucester and two of the King's nurses from Buckingham Palace, who were instructed by the King to tell him all about the show when they returned. The performance that night included yet again the Crazy Gang, who began their comic capers before the royal party arrived, warming up the audience. They then appeared on the stairs as the Queen arrived, dressed as Beefeaters, but they didn't fool Her Majesty. Also in the show was the crazy and lovable Harry Secombe, one of the originators of goon humour. I saw Harry several times in his early days and his comedy has always been very infectious; it spills into the audience and during his years in radio, television and concerts this larger than life character has kept up a continuous barrage of banter. All this, together with a beautiful voice — what a man!

Also in this royal show were Kenneth Horne and Richard Murdoch, who had their own very popular radio series, *Much Binding in the Marsh*, with their regulars Sam Costa, Maurice Denham and company. Kenneth Horne was basically a businessman, an ex-Cambridge Blue at practically all sporting levels who had come into entertainment on meeting Murdoch. When they were in the RAF, they wrote and appeared in the shows together. I could write a lot about Kenneth Horne. I worked with him for the best part of eight years in those marvellous series, *Beyond our Ken* and *Round the Horne*. He was a gifted broadcaster and radio was his natural element. He also compèred *Twenty Questions* and many TV panel games.

At the end of January 1952 the King, with the Queen, Princess Elizabeth, the Duke of Edinburgh and Princess Margaret, went to see *South Pacific* at the Theatre Royal Drury Lane. After the performance the royal party met the cast, including its star, Mary Martin. Also in *South Pacific* playing a minor role was Mary's young son, Larry Hagman. Almost thirty years later the Queen Mother would again meet Mary and her son, who was by this time world famous as 'J. R.' Ewing from the TV serial *Dallas*.

The King went to London Airport to say goodbye to Princess Elizabeth and the Duke of Edinburgh, who were leaving on a trip that was to take them to East Africa, Australia and New Zealand. After seeing them off, the King went back to Sandringham to complete his recovery, but his poor health suddenly caught up with him. He had not been told how serious his illness was. On 5 February he enjoyed a day's shooting in the country, when his reflexes were as sharp as ever, but that night he died in his sleep.

The King had served us well. He had always wanted to do more than he was able to, through the difficult war years and afterwards. George VI had never just been a bystander. He felt for people, and so of course did his Queen. The King had been very much a family man who loved his wife and daughters, and together as a family they had tremendous regard for their subjects. When Princess Elizabeth got married her father was naturally pleased, but sad as well that his daughter was leaving home. He wrote to her after the wedding, saying, 'I can see that you are sublimely happy with Philip, which is right, but don't forget us, is the wish of your everloving and devoted Papa.'[2]

Notes

1. Bebe Daniels and Ben Lyon, *Life with the Lyons* (Odhams Press, 1953).
2. Keith Middlemas, *Life and Times of George VI* (Weidenfeld and Nicolson, 1974).

7

THEATRE ROYAL

King George had become a friend to entertainers and was relaxed in their company. A man who has had good reason to be thankful for the King's friendship is John Counsell, actor/manager/author and himself a friend to hundreds of actors and actresses. How many people have commenced their actor/manager careers by seeing a notice 'Royal Lavatory', and having found the loo, pulled the chain whilst rendering 'God Save the King'? This incident took place at the Theatre Royal Windsor in 1934, when John Counsell became the 'Governor' there for the first time. The notice referred to was on a light switch in the box office, along with other switches that John was investigating — an eccentric start to one man's love affair with a theatre.

The first Theatre Royal in Windsor was built in 1793 and was frequented by George III when he was in residence at the Castle. The King and Queen were provided with armchairs in the theatre and presented with play bills printed on silk. Any left behind in the auditorium after the performance were highly prized as souvenirs by the rest of the audience. George III would command the best artistes of the day to appear before him, and admission prices were reasonable, with boxes at 3s (15 pence), the pit and gallery 2s. and 1s. Eventually a dissenting sect bought the building, turfed out the actors and turned it into a chapel. The citizens of Windsor subscribed enough money to build a new theatre on the site of the present Theatre Royal in 1815, and it continued as a theatre until fire destroyed it in 1908. Sir William Shipley, the owner, a prosperous and public-spirited man, immediately set about building another theatre, the present one, on the site. During the nine-teenth century the original building was visited by members of the Court at Windsor, but there is no indication that Queen Victoria ever attended a performance there. She, as I have mentioned, commanded entertain-ment at the Castle itself during her reign. It was to this lovely castle town that the present owner John Counsell had come. Counsell had for some time in the twenties been part of the Duke of York's camp at Dymchurch in Kent, first as a schoolboy and then as a member of the staff. The Duke of York's camp was a social experiment which had a lasting effect on those who experienced it. The idea was to bring boys from every walk of life together for certain weeks each year — miners' sons, public schoolboys, tradesmen's children and so on — to play and work together side by side. When John Counsell was on the staff he remembers how there would always be a problem getting the boys from different social backgrounds to integrate and mix with one another at first. Counsell had a regular routine to break down these barriers, which he always performed at breakfast on the first day. He would come out of the kitchen into the dining hall carrying about twenty old and chipped plates, and do a 'cod' (theatrical term for false) fall, ending up on the floor in a pile of smashed crockery. The boys, after the initial shock, roared with laughter and the ice was broken. The Duke of York would visit the camp regularly and join in the sporting activities and involve himself in the workshops. He was a mechanically minded man who could mend a watch or put together a wireless set with some ease. Counsell's friendship with the Duke was born out of a mutual understanding of youth in that small Kentish town, and it was to continue through the Duke's reign as King. As a result of his meeting with the Duke, and the Duke's friends, he was able to 'sell' his new ideas for the Windsor theatre in the right circles. Alas, the people of Windsor were generally indifferent to it and in a short time John Counsell had to give up. His dreams were shattered, but even in defeat he was determined to go back someday. Before he had to close the doors in 1934 the Duke and Duchess of York paid a visit to the theatre and thoroughly enjoyed it. The visit had been set up when Counsell got a message to call the Duke at the Castle. He did this, and His Royal Highness told him that he and the Duchess would be popping over and could he tell him what was on. Counsell told the Duke it was a thriller called *The Bat* and proudly added that his little theatre had a Royal Box. The Duke said, 'Oh no, you can't see a thing from a box, I'll have four stall seats, and don't tell anyone we're coming, we want to enjoy an informal evening.' Counsell himself was acting in the play, and at the end of it he went to the front of the house to meet their Royal Highnesses. He found them waiting in the stalls corridor, the manager having mislaid the key to the retiring room. The Duke, sitting on a radiator, was enthusiastic about the play, and said that it was a wonderful thing for Windsor to have such a good repertory company, and that he hoped to come again often, and come again he did, as King. John Counsell, as he had promised himself, re-opened the Theatre Royal in 1938, but only after the most exhaustive, complicated and nerve-racking search for 'Angels' (financial backers).

Within a few weeks of Counsell's re-opening of the theatre, George VI and Queen Elizabeth, with four guests, including Clement Attlee, who was to become the immediate post-war Labour Prime Minister of this country, attended a performance of *The Rose Without a Thorn*, the sad story of Catherine Howard and Henry VIII. The King had asked for six 3/6d. front balcony seats. Can you imagine the excitement and apprehension that John and his staff and actors must have felt on this night, the first time a reigning monarch and his Queen were to be entertained by Counsell's Windsor Repertory Company? On the walk to the auditorium the Queen told John how pleased she and the King were that he had managed to re-open the theatre: 'We have been telling everybody about it.' Their majesties obviously enjoyed *Rose Without a Thorn*, and as they left the Queen said, 'We are determined that your company must succeed this time, and please don't hesitate to let us know if there is anything we can do to help.' Apart from anything else, the Press made capital out of the fact that the monarch had sat in 3/6d. seats, so their majesties' visit was just the help that Counsell needed, and their presence on that night ensured the future success of the Windsor Theatre.

In 1939 the big production at the theatre was *Pygmalion*; King George and Queen Elizabeth arranged to bring a large party to see it, including Queen Mary and the Duke and Duchess of Gloucester. Queen Elizabeth introduced John to Queen Mary, and the old Queen said, 'Are you the manager of this theatre?' Counsell said he was. The Queen obviously wanted to know who she should address any complaints to if she had any. Counsell overheard the King say to his mother, 'Yes, Mama, he is one of my boys from the camp, but that does not mean he is an amateur.' Queen Mary, together with the rest of the royal party, loved the play, and when it was over she had a long chat with Mary Kerridge, who played Eliza Doolittle, and afterwards said to Counsell, 'That girl has a future, and I know what I'm talking about.'

During the war the theatre survived under the guidance of Oliver Gordon and Mary Kerridge, who had become Counsell's wife in 1939. When John came back to take over the reins after his considerable war service, one of his first productions was Noël Coward's *This Happy Breed*. George VI and Queen Elizabeth came to see it, their first visit to the theatre since 1939, and brought Princess Margaret with them. On the night of their visit the carefully planned cueing of the National Anthem at the start of the play went slightly awry, much to the embarrassment of Counsell, but the Queen helped to save the situation when she laid her hand on John's arm and said, 'Please don't worry, it's all in the spirit of the evening.' The play started prematurely, and in the darkness the King used his cigarette lighter to search for the number of his seat. Meanwhile Noël Coward, who had come down to Windsor for the performance, was standing at the top of the stairs with the Queen. Coward said, 'Go on, Ma'am, go on.' Her Majesty said, 'I would like to go on, Mr Coward, but you're standing on my dress.' Apparently that incident was a source of amusement to the Royal Family for a long time.

The following year the King and Queen saw *Arsenic and Old Lace* at the theatre, and when they arrived the King was told the form for the evening was as before, to which he replied, 'You mean you're going to turn the lights out on us again.' Many years later when Queen Elizabeth, then the Queen Mother, was in the audience, she spotted Noël Coward and remarked to him, 'Good evening, Mr Coward, I'm wearing a perfectly splendid dress for standing on!' The last time George VI visited the theatre at Windsor was in 1950 to see *Off the Record*. The Queen had been driving past in the afternoon and had seen that the play was being presented, and remembering how much some other members of the Royal Family had enjoyed seeing it in London, enquired if there were any seats left. The Queen insisted that no one should be deprived of their booking if it was sold out, but as luck would have it the royal seats in the middle of the balcony stalls were still free. It was an impromptu visit, and in the interval the King chatted to Counsell about all the good work that had been done at Windsor.

Queen Elizabeth II and the Duke of Edinburgh went to the theatre in 1955 to see *Witness for the Prosecution*. The Queen and Duke were delighted with what they saw, and both went on to the stage after the performance to meet Agatha Christie, the cast and staff. The next production was a type of musical revue called *The World's the Limit*, which starred Beryl Reid, Peter Graves and Patrick Cargill, with music and lyrics by Ronnie Hill and Julian More. The Queen took her entire Ascot house party to see the show, and when John Counsell told a friend about the forthcoming visit, the friend said, 'Oh, a coach party booking, eh.' When Her Majesty arrived at the theatre she told Counsell how much she had enjoyed *Witness for the Prosecution*, which she had seen a month previously, and that she and the Duke were delighted to be able to bring her house party this time, as it was a convenient way of entertaining them. It was probably the largest royal party that had ever attended a theatre privately. Apart from the Queen and the Duke of Edinburgh there was the Queen Mother, Princess Margaret, the Duke and Duchess of Gloucester, the Duchess of Kent and Princess Alexandra. Two years later the Queen took over almost the entire theatre to see a new play, *Four in Hand*. Apart from Her Majesty's house guests she also brought along many of her personal friends, household staff and local people connected with activities that the Royal Family were interested in. There was a great feeling of informality about the evening. When the royal party was

Theatre Royal, Windsor. *By courtesy of John Counsell*

making its way to the auditorium the orchestra was playing a waltz, and quite spontaneously the Duke of Edinburgh took the Queen Mother's hand and danced her down the corridor. In the interval the Queen said how marvellous it was to see all her friends together and obviously enjoying themselves.

In 1956, after much preparation, the musical *Grab Me a Gondola* was produced at Windsor, with great success. There were rave revues in abundance, and on some nights the curtain calls would last as long as eight minutes. The Queen, the Queen Mother and Princess Margaret saw the production there, setting the seal, as John Counsell said, on the Windsor Theatre's greatest triumph. The musical eventually transferred to Shaftesbury Avenue, where it ran for a long time.

In 1965 refurbishing and decorating took place, and when it was re-opened with *The Rivals* Her Majesty the Queen was in the audience. In April 1980 no less than three reigning monarchs attended a performance at the theatre on Garter Monday: Her Majesty the Queen, the Queen of Denmark and the Grand Duke of Luxembourg. John Counsell's dreams and ambitions in the thirties have become a reality in his lifetime, and that superb little theatre at Windsor has written his name into theatrical history for ever.

8

'OH, WHAT A NIGHT IT WAS...'

The young Queen Elizabeth II began her reign on the tarmac of Entebbe Airport — an airport that was to gain notoriety many years later for a daring raid by Israeli Commandos on a hijacked aeroplane. The Queen was in East Africa when the news of her father's death reached her. George VI had left his daughter a legacy of his fine example as a monarch. With all the enormous responsibility that had suddenly come to Queen Elizabeth, and at the same time coping with her own and her mother's personal grief, she still had time for the theatre once the period of Court mourning was over. The Queen had with Prince Philip the added responsibility of bringing up two young children in the family circle; the family unit was as important to them as it had been to George VI.

Her Majesty's first visit to the theatre as reigning sovereign was to see *The Young Elizabeth* at the Criterion in July 1952. Other visits by members of the Royal Family to the theatre included performances of *Call Me Madam*, Emlyn Williams' one-man show of Charles Dickens readings, *Rigoletto* at Covent Garden, and the pantomime *Jack and Jill* at the Casino.

The Royal Variety Performance at the Palladium was of course the first Her Majesty had attended since her accession. It included Vic Oliver, the American comedian who had made his home over here since appearing with Bebe Daniels and Ben Lyon in *Hi Gang*. He gained a certain amount of notoriety when he married Winston Churchill's daughter Sarah. Also appearing was Australian juggler Rob Murray, who used to mutter under his breath all through his act, and the tenor Joseph Locke, whose song 'Goodbye' from *White Horse Inn* had audiences shouting for more. The great French entertainer Maurice Chevalier was present, as was Tony Hancock, whose brilliant comedy on radio and television is still appreciated today.

Norman Wisdom in this performance showed everyone why he had become a star in four short years. His comic and eccentric playing of various musical instruments was complemented by a very warm and endearing singing voice. In this show Norman was sharing a dressing-room with several other comedians, including Ted Ray, Jerry Desmonde

John Tiller's company of dancers in the 1950s. The Tiller Girls have appeared in many Royal Variety Performances since their inception nearly 50 years ago. *Photograph courtesy of Maureen Robins*

(of Sid Field fame) and Tony Hancock. Tony Hancock sat at the dressing-room table making up very slowly, not saying much to anyone, but every few minutes he would have a glass of brandy. This went on for some time and eventually Wisdom, who is practically a teetotaller, said to Hancock that he thought he'd had enough, and perhaps he wouldn't be capable to perform. Hancock said he was OK and had another swig. Eventually he got his call and went out of the dressing-room to make his way to the stage. All those left in the dressing-room listened to the tannoy and held their breath, worried that Tony was not going to be able to perform properly. They needn't have worried. Tony Hancock was a great success, and when he returned to the dressing-room he didn't say anything when Norman Wisdom and the others congratulated him, went straight to the bottle of brandy, finished it off, took his coat and went out to find a pub while he was waiting for the finale line-up.

At yet another royal show Norman teamed up for a double bit with Bruce Forsyth, at the end of which Wisdom had to exit off-stage first.

At the dress rehearsal he started to leave the stage doing an eccentric dance step. Bruce said to him, 'What are you doing now?' Norman said, 'I'm trucking off.' Lew Grade (now Lord Grade), who was watching in the stalls, jumped up and said, 'Norman, you can't say that in the show, it might be misheard.' How careful you have to be.

Once when Norman Wisdom was opening a big garden fête at Hatfield House attended by many notables, the guest of honour was Queen Elizabeth the Queen Mother. It was a wet afternoon and Norman, dressed in his famous gump suit, was sheltering with many of the guests under a gigantic open-sided marquee. Norman noticed that one side of the marquee was sagging under the weight of rain-water. The little devil came out in Norman and he pushed his hand up into the canvas, spilling several gallons of water over the edge on to the top-hatted guests standing round the outside of the tent. The Queen Mother, who had been looking through the French windows of the house, had seen Norman's action, and when Her Majesty came out to meet some of the guests, she said to Norman, 'I saw what you did just now, you little tinker.' Norman Wisdom's films have, I think, been some of the funniest ever made in this country, and one has to remember they have been successfully received abroad, too. I have always been a fan of Wisdom's, ever since I first saw him in a variety bill at the London Casino in 1948. That bill was topped by American singer Alan Jones, whose 'Donkey Serenade' is still played in various record programmes. Alan's son Jack has done pretty well for himself too, one way and another.

In 1953 the Queen had her own production to oversee, the Coronation. Television's biggest production to date, with up to twenty cameras covering the ceremony itself, it was seen by millions of people at home and abroad. A Coronation present to the nation was the conquest of Everest by Edmund Hilary and Sherpa Tensing. Early in the year there was a sad occasion for the Royal Family and the nation with the death of Queen Mary. Queen Mary was one of the most theatrically knowledgeable of the whole family. Through the twenties and thirties she had patronised the theatre in many ways and this had continued in her later years with such varied fare as *Charley's Aunt, The Paragon, Annie Get Your Gun*, the hilarious comedy *One Wild Oat* and many visits to the smaller club theatres such as the New Lindsey, the Boltons and the Gateway. Queen Mary had played a big part in stabilising the monarchy after the abdication of her eldest son. She was known personally by many shop-keepers and was a discerning customer who looked for quality and value. She was a regular customer of Marks and Spencer stores at one time. A dutiful wife to George V and his strength in many ways, she knew the

King liked to have her at home for afternoon tea and always did her best to see that she was there to pour his first cup. In Coronation year the Queen's visits to the theatre were as usual varied. With the Duke of Edinburgh she went to the first night of *Henry VIII* at the Old Vic, and together with the Queen Mother and Princess Margaret saw a charity performance of *Aren't We All*. The musical *Guys and Dolls* and revues *Airs on a Shoestring* and *Intimacy at Eight Thirty* were also honoured with royal visits. The Queen, the Duke of Edinburgh and Princess Margaret attended the Coronation year Royal Variety Performance at the Coliseum in November.

One of the stars of this show was Jimmy James. Now there was a funny man. Although a teetotaller, James was one of the finest stage drunks you've ever seen. A sample of Jimmy's brilliant situations with his stooges would start with one of them appearing in ridiculous clothes carrying a box. James, who knew that he was going to be involved in another bout of lunacy, began to humour the intruder and eventually accepted the ridiculous situation.

> *Stooge* (Conyers): When I was in the Diplomatic Service I was given this elephant.
>
> *James*: Where do you keep it?
>
> *Conyers*: In this box.
>
> *James*: Is it male or female?
>
> *Conyers*: No, an elephant.
>
> *James*: I don't suppose it makes any difference whether it's male or female.
>
> *Stooge* (Eli): It wouldn't make any difference to anyone except another elephant.
>
> *James* (to Eli): I shall have to stop you going to these youth clubs.

When you watched this group at work you got caught up in the lunacy, but it was a joy to be part of it. Jimmy James was also very funny off-stage, unusual for a comedian. His son, James Casey, who played Conyers with his father at one time and is now head of BBC Radio Comedy in Manchester, told me that his father could be walking down the road and quite suddenly would go up to a complete stranger and hail him as a long-lost friend he hadn't seen for years. There would then ensue a conversation discussing families and so on, which Jimmy made so convincing that the stranger would eventually believe he knew James personally. Jimmy would finish off the conversation by saying to the unsuspecting stranger, 'I remember you lent me a quid twenty years ago and I've not forgotten, here it is, buy your missus a bunch of flowers.' He would then move on as if nothing had happened. Jimmy was a great comic to be with.

The Queen, the Duke of Edinburgh, Princess Margaret, the Queen Mother and the Crown Prince and Princess of Norway attended a performance of Benjamin Britten's opera *Gloriana* at Covent Garden in 1953, and an unusual theatrical event took place in a charity performance at the Palladium about this time: Noël Coward, Laurence Olivier and John Gielgud appeared doing a dance routine as three Teddy boys.

A large number of theatrical productions were visited by the Queen and other members of the Royal Family during the early years of Her Majesty's reign, including *The Boy Friend, The King and I*, the 550th performance of *The Mousetrap*, Terence Rattigan's *Separate Tables* and a performance of *The Frog*, co-directed by Princess Margaret for an amateur company at the Scala Theatre.

At the 25th Royal Variety Performance in 1954 Bob Hope topped the bill, and what can one say about this remarkable American comedian that hasn't all been said before? He is nearly eighty years old, has a brain as sharp as a razor, and has been an enormous success in every medium of show business. He's a better than average golfer and he promotes the Bob Hope Golf Classics all over the world to raise money for charity. His professional technique is faultless. At the beginning of his act the spotlight settles on the wings, the orchestra strikes up with his signature tune 'Thanks for the Memory', and then, with the audience kept waiting just long enough to almost bring them to their feet in anticipation, he emerges to start his casual walk to the centre of the stage and begin his barrage of topical jokes — some so topical that he reads them off cards held by someone in the orchestra pit. Not so long ago, when he was in another Royal Variety Show, the line-up at the final rehearsal was practising the National Anthem. Another American, impressionist Rich Little, said to Hope, 'I don't know the words.' Bob said, 'Don't worry, just watch the Queen's lips, I'm sure she knows it.'

There were two Royal Variety performances in 1955, one at Blackpool in April — outside the capital for the first time. There were many established favourites in the Blackpool show, including organist Reginald Dixon, a great favourite in the resort with his many years' residence at the Tower Ballroom and easily recognisable with his signature tune 'I do Like to be Beside the Seaside', Jimmy Jewel and Ben Warris, then firmly established as one of the great double acts of the post-war period, Charlie Cairoli and Paul, the musical clowns from the Tower Circus in Blackpool, George Formby and American singing star Eddie Fisher, who can count Elizabeth Taylor and Debbie Reynolds amongst his wives. In the show too were those great slapstick comics Lauri Lupino Lane and George Truzzi. These two had the paper-hanging routine down to a fine art. It had all the ingredients so worthy of the great Lupino theatrical family going back many years. People have tried to copy it and better it, but it's just superb as it is. It's all built round two people trying to paste a piece of wallpaper on to a wall with different coloured paste. At the end of it anyone involved in it has to have a bath before carrying on in the show. Norman Vaughan and I once did this routine twice daily for the entire run of a pantomime.

The London Royal Variety Performance was held at the Victoria Palace, with Johnny Ray in the cast. I saw the opening night of his Palladium season and to quote a line from one of his songs, 'Oh, What a Night it was, it Really was'. His most famous song, 'Cry', had even the hardened theatre-goer going wild. Outside the Palladium teenagers packing Argyll Street and the area round the stage door were hysterical, embracing one another, screaming and banging their fists on the pavement. I believe it was the first uninhibited fan adulation that this country had experienced.

Jimmy Edwards was featured in a funny sketch, 'Judge for Yourself', with other well known personalities including Richard Attenborough and Diana Dors. Edwards played the judge, and his buffoonery made a mockery of bewigged honours. When he asked a defendant how he pleaded and the defendant went to pieces, Judge Jim said, 'Oh, you are a miserable pleader.' The uncensored version of this sketch was a riot. Jim is a delightfully larger than life character who has been entertaining audiences with his scholastic humour and musical nonsense ever since he was discovered at the Windmill Theatre many years ago. Dave King should be mentioned here, because his appearance in this 1955 performance came about as a result of his quick rise to fame via the medium of television. He was completely unknown when he was given six minutes in a BBC television programme in 1954, and he certainly made the most of it with his impressions of John Wayne, Robert Mitchum and his own great style in comedy. In the last few years he has established himself as a very good straight actor.

There is no doubt that the big entertainment event of 1955 in this country was the commencement of commercial television. It opened up a battle between the BBC and the companies of independent television for viewers who up to that time had had no choice. Of course competition is always good, but those awful words 'Programme Rating Figures' soon came into being. One of the big trump cards in the early days of commercial television was *Sunday Night at the London Palladium*, a weekly live show. It had a compère, a game called 'Beat the Clock' with good prizes, and guest celebrities from all over the world. The early compères for this show were Tommy Trinder, Bruce Forsyth, a young Scots comedian Don Arrol, and Norman Vaughan.

The Crazy Gang — Eddie Gray, Teddy Knox, Jimmy Nervo, Charlie Naughton, Jimmy Gold and Bud Flanagan rehearsing a burlesque of *A Midsummer Night's Dream* for the Royal Variety Performance at the Palladium that never was, 1956. *Photograph courtesy of BBC Hulton Picture Library*

Nineteen fifty-six brought an international crisis that unseated a Prime Minister. During that year there were royal visits to the ballet, including the Bolshoi, pantomime, opera at Glyndbourne, French revue and a number of plays. The crisis I've mentioned came towards the end of the year, when at the very last minute the Suez débâcle prevented the Royal Variety Performance from taking place. At that time I had my bags packed ready to leave with a CSE (Combined Services Entertainment) unit to tour various bases in the Middle East. I was told it was cancelled about 4 p.m. in the afternoon. At the same moment Val Parnell walked into the stalls of the London Palladium just as the cast for that night's royal performance was finishing rehearsals. He had to tell them that owing to

Notice being put up outside the Palladium announcing the cancellation of the 1956 Royal Variety Performance. *Photograph courtesy of BBC Hulton Picture Library*

the international situation in the Middle East the show was cancelled. The cast were of course stunned. Gracie Fields tried to comfort some of her colleagues who were naturally distressed that they were to be denied the chance of appearing before Her Majesty.

Max Bygraves recalled to me the feelings of some of the performers on that afternoon:

I was sharing a dressing-room with Liberace and he was heartbroken — he had travelled overland from Los Angeles and by sea from New York to Southampton — in all, it had taken nine days because, at that time, neither he nor his mother liked flying. He wept openly and several of us stood around not really able to do anything. Amongst us was Jimmy Wheeler, the Cockney comedian, and after commiserating long enough, he took his violin out of the case and said in his fruity delivery, 'I've rehearsed this bloody act for a fortnight so somebody's gonna hear it.' He then went into the routine, he asked Liberace to sit on the wash basin and pretended it was the Royal Box, he addressed all his gags to the American pianist and they were jokes that would *never* have been passed by the Lord Chamberlain. Suddenly we were all laughing, the disaster had become hysteria; Winifred Atwell decided we should all go back to her place and open a bottle or two of champagne, which we did.

And the last I remember of that night was leaving her house around 4 a.m. with Winnie and Liberace sitting at the grand piano playing 'Chopsticks'.

BBC Television celebrated its 21st anniversary in November 1957, a service that was becoming second to none in the world. The legitimate theatre in the West End had not yet been affected by the growth of television, and was still profitable to managements and a source of entertainment for those who patronised it, including members of the Royal Family.

The Royal Variety Performance at the Palladium caused one young agent some concern. The show included the Crazy Gang in a scene from their current production *These Foolish Kings*, and the young Bob Monkhouse, who has stayed the course remarkably well and has probably fronted more quiz shows for television than anybody else. Comedian Dickie Henderson was making his royal début just 31 years after his father Dick Henderson made his first appearance in a royal performance. Scots entertainer Jimmy Logan appeared that night, and also Judy Garland, who won over the mink and sabled audience completely. A production number called 'Variety' included practically every popular artiste of the day, and topping the bill was American singing star Mario Lanza: he was the person who caused the problems for agent Peter Prichard.

Peter, now a successful artistes manager with his own company, was for many years on the staff of the Lew and Leslie Grade agency organisation. The Grades, who became one of the largest agencies in show business, have been known to nearly every professional performer in the world, and I believe a good deal of the general public as well. When Peter Prichard was working for them one of his duties was to look after the stars the agency had booked into this country or other parts of Europe. One of these assignments was to look after Mario Lanza, and Prichard practically lived with him while he was working outside America. They were based in Rome for some time in 1957 when Lanza was invited to appear in the Royal Variety Show. As I have mentioned, it was a star-studded cast, but through the popularity of his films and records Mario Lanza was quite naturally the biggest attraction on the night. Lanza, along with Prichard, had been booked into the Dorchester Hotel for the week-end and Peter had instructions not to let him out of his sight. Lanza had a reputation for heavy bouts of drinking (and over-eating) and being a little free with his fists when the mood took him. He was genuinely very nervous about appearing in front of a live audience on stage, and this naturally made him edgy. It was arranged to have the theatre cleared on the afternoon before the show of all but a skeleton staff so that Lanza could rehearse with the orchestra on his own. Other artistes were told to stay in their dressing-rooms until the singer had finished. Prichard got to the Palladium, put Lanza in his dressing-room and then told Val Parnell and Charles Henry the director that all was ready. He went back to the dressing-room and, to his astonishment, at that point a photographer from the *Musical Express* appeared from nowhere, came into the dressing-room and started to take pictures. Lanza went berserk, told Peter that he'd been promised privacy and proceeded to punch him on the nose. Peter, rather upset about this treatment, told Val Parnell that he'd had enough and was leaving. Parnell begged Peter to stay and keep quiet about the incident until after the show next day. Somehow or other the *Daily Mirror* got hold of the incident and Peter's home telephone number and rang there. His grandmother was the only one at home, and she knew nothing about the Palladium incident. When the reporter asked her if Peter had been in a fight she said, 'Oh, very likely, he's always getting into trouble with the kids around here.' It was a long time since Peter had been a 'kid'.

During the interval of the performance on the Monday night Hugh Cudlipp, the *Daily Mirror* boss, asked Val Parnell whether the story of the punch-up was true. Parnell replied, 'Of course not, you can see Prichard if you want to, he hasn't a mark on him.' Whether Cudlipp believed Parnell or not, he didn't print the story. A postscript to the Mario Lanza incident occurred in the line-up presentation after the show to meet Her

Majesty the Queen and Prince Philip. His Royal Highness said to Lanza, 'I hear you are on a European tour at the moment, I hope it's proving successful.' Lanza replied, 'If you call five thousand dollars a night successful, yes, and what's your story?' A very strange remark to make to anyone, but the Duke dealt with it beautifully. He said, 'Oh my story is about as interesting as my voice,' and passed on to meet other artistes.

In 1958 the Queen attended two Royal Variety performances, as she had done in 1955, one in London in November and one in Glasgow in July. The Scottish show was unique in that it was the first Variety Performance ever to be held there. A Royal Command due to be given in the presence of George V in 1911 had to be cancelled due to a fire at the Empire Palace Theatre in Edinburgh. Glasgow was going to make up for the delay in staging the royal occasion that Scotland missed 47 years earlier.

9

THE SCOTTISH CONNECTION

The Alhambra Theatre Glasgow had never looked better than it did on the night of 3 July 1958. For Stewart Cruickshank, the managing director of the Alhambra, it was a very special evening. His family had made the theatrical empire of Howard and Wyndham a great one, not only in Scotland but also south of the Border. One of the theatres owned by the company in Edinburgh had actually been built by an earlier generation of Cruickshank's family. I could not possibly list all the performers taking part, and I'm sure the British, American and Continental artistes will forgive me if I give my attention to the home team. Wee Alec Finlay, actor and writer Rikki Fulton, impressionist Margot Henderson, the husband and wife comedy act of Clarke and Murray, the bright young Scots entertainer Jimmy Logan, singer Kenneth McKellar, who has conquered the south just as successfully as Scotland, Jack Radcliffe, Alistair McHarg, the elegant and popular singer Robert Wilson, comedian Tommy Morgan, Stanley Baxter, who nowadays presents some wonderful television spectaculars, the City of Glasgow Police Pipe Band, and Jimmy Shand and his Band. Jimmy Shand has entertained at many private parties during his years in the profession, including some at the royal residences of Windsor Castle, Balmoral and Holyrood Palace. When Jimmy received his MBE from Her Majesty the Queen in 1962 he was wearing formal morning dress. The Queen said to him, 'I thought you'd be wearing the kilt.'

The Alhambra Theatre was completely redecorated for this royal performance — its first face-lift in forty years. The Royal Box was decorated in scarlet velvet with pink roses and carnations. The chairs in the Royal Box were gold and pale blue of eighteenth-century French design. The trumpeters of the Black Watch on stage heralded the arrival of Her Majesty and His Royal Highness the Duke of Edinburgh into the Royal Box. The whole show, which was produced by a familiar figure in spectacular staging, Dick Hurran, was brought to its glittering conclusion by the Band of the Scots Guards leading the audience in 'Scotland the Brave'. Without doubt the first official Scottish Royal Variety Performance had been an unqualified success. The history of royal

BALMORAL CASTLE,

MONDAY, 16th SEPTEMBER, 1895,

An Original Comedy in Four Acts,

BY

R. C. CARTON,

ENTITLED—

LIBERTY HALL.

Mr. Owen, - - -	MR. GEORGE ALEXANDER
William Todman, - - - -	MR. E. M. ROBSON
Hon. Gerald Harringay, -	MR. ALLAN AYNESWORTH
Mr. Pedrick (Solicitor), - -	MR. ARTHUR ROYSTON
J. Briginshaw, - - - - -	MR. H. H. VINCENT
Robert Binks (Todman's Shop Boy), -	MASTER JONES
Luscombe, - - - - -	MR. FRANK DYALL
Mr. Hickson, { Brother and	MR. F. KINSEY PEILE
Miss Hickson, { Sister, }	MISS WINIFRED DOLAN
Crafer (Todman's Servant), - -	MISS M. MOUILLOT
Amy Chilworth, { Daughters of the late	MISS FURTADO CLARKE
Blanche Chilworth, { Sir Norman Chilworth, }	MISS EVELYN MILLARD

Programme for *Liberty Hall*, Balmoral Castle, September 1895. *By courtesy of Theatre Museum* theatrical events in Scotland is considerable, and I would like to recall some of them.

Rizzio, secretary to Mary Queen of Scots, had a friend in Italy who was a popular minstrel in that country, and mentioned this fact to the Queen. She thought she would like to be entertained by this talented friend of Rizzio's and commanded him to Holyrood Palace. Before he arrived, however, his friend Rizzio was murdered by the Queen's husband, Lord Darnley. This story of possibly one of the first theatrical commands in Scotland has no confirmation, but if it is true I wonder what happened to the minstrel: did he hear the news of his friend's murder when he arrived in this country and, deciding it was rather far to return to Italy without having achieved anything, stay and get employment in some other part of the country?

In 1601 Mary's son James VI commanded a Shakespearian performance in Aberdeen, and it is possible that the Bard himself was one of the players. It had been a long time since a British sovereign had set foot on Scottish soil when in 1822 George IV landed at Leith on his way to Edinburgh where he was given a great welcome, and very soon his ability to please endeared him to the whole city. Among other events, the King gave a dinner party at Holyrood Palace and the entertainment during the banquet was provided by 'Gow's Celebrated Band', playing favourite Scottish airs. During his visit the King saw a performance of *Rob Roy* at the Theatre Royal in Shakespeare Square, the site now occupied by the General Post Office in Edinburgh, and a pleasing part of this production for His Majesty was the singing of 'My Love is like a Red, Red Rose'.

Nearly all the royal theatrical events in the nineteenth century took place at Balmoral, the summer residence of the sovereign, but in fact the first command in Deeside was by the Prince of Wales at Abergeldie Castle. Queen Victoria came over from Balmoral for the evening — her first theatrical entertainment since Prince Albert's death. In 1891 the Queen herself commanded a performance of *The Mikado* to Balmoral and this was almost certainly the first theatrical command to the Castle home. Through the 1890s many drama productions were taken to Balmoral with such names as Sir Squire and Lady Bancroft, Beerbohm Tree and George Alexander. Alexander had a number of plays for Her Majesty to choose from and she selected *Liberty Hall*, a harmless piece with no possible offence. The ballroom at Balmoral is small; to erect a stage big enough for a touring set and still leave room for an audience must have taken some doing. The Queen sat in the front row holding a little bell which she tinkled when she was ready for the curtain to rise on each act. The cast, after being presented to Her Majesty, was given a 'Royal' supper. It was pouring with rain when they were ready to leave in the

The set for Act One of *Liberty Hall*, Balmoral Castle, September 1895. *By courtesy of Theatre Museum*

early hours of the following morning on their way back to Ballater Station, so the Queen had the carriages brought round to the front of the Castle, as there was quite a long walk from the rear entrance to the vehicles and the performers would have had to sit in wet clothes for a long time. A thoughtful gesture from the ageing Queen. The company's next date at the Lyceum Edinburgh was a sell-out due to the publicity of the Balmoral Command. It was at the Castle that the Queen's children in their young days used to act out plays themselves. There were commands by George V to Balmoral during his reign, and he favoured giving Scottish repertory companies an opportunity to perform there, which of course was a great boost for that type of theatre. The King once asked an actor whether it was true that on one occasion they had dressed in a pig-sty? The actor replied, 'Yes, but they were pedigree pigs, Sir.' The King thought this remark very funny. He was most charming to everyone, as was Queen Mary, and they both made sure that the cast had a good supper before leaving.

Sir Harry Lauder was commanded by King George and Queen Mary to give a special performance at Balmoral in the twenties, and on this occasion their majesties presented Lauder and his wife with two silver-framed photographs, each of them autographed.

The Perth and Dundee repertory companies were invited to Balmoral by George VI, and it must have been of great interest to Queen Elizabeth, as her family home at Glamis Castle is not far from both these cities. Glamis was the scene of a royal occasion on 21 August 1935 when the Earl and Countess of Strathmore, Queen Elizabeth the Queen Mother's parents, gave a fifth birthday party for Princess Margaret. A Miss Bertha Wadell and her company of Glasgow children's theatre were commanded to provide the entertainment. Miss Wadell's theatre was specially designed for children, and she became a great favourite of the Royal Family, later appearing with her company at Buckingham Palace. After the party at Glamis on her birthday Princess Margaret was asked what she liked best: she said, 'The clowns and the sausages.' The clowns had been part of the entertainment.

The Gillies' Ball at Balmoral has been a feature of the Royal Family's summer holidays there for many years. The bands for these balls have during the last thirty years been provided by the Sinclair family, mother, father, and then later by their son Jack. Sinclair has also appeared recently in a Command Performance at the Beach Ballroom Aberdeen. He is very proud of the fact that he has in the past arranged country dance parties for Prince Charles and Princess Anne so that they could be better acquainted with all aspects of Scottish dancing. Along with Sinclair and Jimmy Shand and his Band, Jim Macleod has also been prominent in appearing at Balmoral during the past few years. I recently met Jim at the beautiful Dunblane Hydro, near Stirling, where he is resident entertainments manager. He broadcasts regularly from the Hydro for BBC Radio's *The Kilt is my Delight* programme. Her Majesty the Queen told Macleod that she was a regular listener to this series.

Edinburgh, for the past fifty years at any rate, has seen many royal theatrical occasions, both formal and informal. George V and Queen Mary, with the Duke and Duchess of York, saw *The Admirable Crichton* at the Lyceum Theatre in 1931. The King and Queen paid another visit to the Lyceum in 1934 to see Pinero's *Enchanted Cottage*. On this occasion the front of the theatre was garlanded with flowers, and people thronged the route, leaning out of windows in the high tenement buildings. One eyewitness recalled the sound of cheering from the east end of Grindley Street shortly after eight o'clock and a cry of 'Here they come!' As the

Opposite: silk programme for *Rob Roy*, Royal Lyceum Theatre, Edinburgh, October 1962.

Royal Lyceum Theatre

EDINBURGH

Proprietor Mr Meyer Oppenheim   Managing Agents Messrs Howard & Wyndham Ltd   Manager Mr Charles T. Tripp

GALA PERFORMANCE

IN HONOUR OF

His Majesty The King of Norway

AND IN THE PRESENCE OF

Her Majesty The Queen

AND

His Royal Highness The Duke of Edinburgh

WEDNESDAY 17th October 1962 at 7.30 o'clock

"ROB ROY"

Presented by

MR MEYER OPPENHEIM

A National Drama with music by Mr ISACK POCOCK
based on the novel by Sir WALTER SCOTT *Revised by Messrs* ROBERT KEMP
and GERARD SLEVIN *Original lyrics by Mr* ROBERT KEMP
Music arranged and original music composed by Mr CEDRIC THORPE DAVIE

CHARACTERS IN ORDER OF APPEARANCE

Andrew Fairservice	Mr JAMES GIBSON	Mr PAUL KERMACK	Johson
Sir Frederick Vernon	Mr DAVID STEUART	Mr JOHN YOUNG	Major Galbraith
Diana Vernon	Miss PAMELA KAY	Mr BRYDEN MURDOCH	MacStuart
Rashleigh Osbaldistone	Mr JOHN CAIRNEY	Miss JEAN TAYLOR SMITH	Jean MacAlpine
Francis Osbaldistone	Mr ANDREW DOWNIE	Mr MICHAEL O'HALLORAN	Captain Thornton
Rob Roy MacGregor	Mr ARCHIE DUNCAN	Mr LESLIE WRIGHT	Sergeant
Mattie	Miss MORAG FORSYTH	Mr JOHN TOYE	Corporal
Bailie Nicol Jarvie	Mr CALLUM MILL	Miss LENNOX MILNE	Helen MacGregor
Saunders Wylie	Mr BROWN DERBY	Mr PAUL KERMACK	Alastair
Dougal	Mr WALTER CARR	Mr IAN FRASER } sons of Rob Roy { Robert
Mr Owen	Mr CHRISTOPHER PAGE	Mr KEITH RICHARDSON } { Hamish

CHORUS: *Soldiers, Highlanders, Townspeople*

Directed by Mr GERARD SLEVIN

Settings by Miss ANNE CARRICK *and Messrs* SEAN KENNY LTD

Fights arranged by Mr PETER DIAMOND

Orchestra and Chorus under the direction of Mr RICHARD TELFER

Production under the supervision of Mr DENNIS RAMSDEN

NORWEGIAN NATIONAL ANTHEM   *GOD SAVE THE QUEEN*

ACT ONE   ACT TWO

The Garden of Osbaldistone Hall	SCENE 1	SCENE 1	Jean MacAlpine's change house at Aberfoyle
A Northumberland hillside at night	SCENE 2	SCENE 2	The Clachan of Aberfoyle
The Garden of Osbaldistone Hall	SCENE 3	SCENE 3	The Pass of Lochard
Glasgow	SCENE 4	SCENE 4	The Hillside
Bailie Nicol Jarvie's house	SCENE 5	SCENE 5	Jean MacAlpine's change house at Aberfoyle
Glasgow Tolbooth	SCENE 6	SCENE 6	Rob Roy's Cave
Glasgow	SCENE 7		

There will be an INTERVAL of 20 minutes at the end of ACT ONE

NORWEGIAN NATIONAL ANTHEM   *GOD SAVE THE QUEEN*

large limousine drew nearer it was seen to contain Sir Harry Lauder, who was to be one of the guests that night at the theatre, and the reception for him was a very warm one, just as it was for George V and Queen Mary when they arrived. A variety show at the Empire Theatre was attended by the Duke and Duchess of York on 2 December 1936. The Duke could not have imagined on that night that in a few days' time he would be King, following his brother's abdication.

A great friend and colleague of mine in *Dad's Army*, actor John Le Mesurier, was in the cast of the Howard and Wyndham Repertory Company's production of *The Romantic Young Lady* in Edinburgh and a royal visitor to the theatre was the lovely Duchess of Kent. The review in the newspaper at the time said, 'John Le Mesurier was a fluent and elegant hero of the open window romance, who could throw his straw hat through it with great flair.' John has made a success of many things in his career, but I didn't know throwing hats through windows was one of them!

The Queen Mother, as Queen, attended some of the Edinburgh Festival productions at the Lyceum, including *Così fan tutte*, in 1949, and after meeting the cast at the end of the performance she drove back to Holyrood Palace. Half an hour later she drove out again to see a performance of *The Gentle Shepherd* at the Edinburgh Royal High School. Every year at least two or three productions are visited by members of the Royal Family during the Festival season in the city. In October 1962 the Queen, the Duke of Edinburgh, Princess Margaret and Lord Snowdon, accompanied by Lord Home, saw a performance of *Rob Roy*. The visit was in honour of King Olav of Norway, who was with the royal party on that night.

Royal visits to the theatre of Glasgow have not been so frequent as in Edinburgh, but nevertheless they have been of significance during the reign of our present Queen. The proposed 1963 Royal Variety Performance at the Alhambra, Glasgow, was marred by internal dissension. Some time before the performance was due to take place, many of the Scottish artistes invited to take part realised that they were going to be relegated to nothing more than a chorus appearance, whereas the English and American artistes were being given solo spots in the production. As most of the Scottish performers were stars in their own right, they decided to withdraw from the show altogether. It was consequently cancelled, and in its place the Queen and the Duke of Edinburgh saw a performance of the *Half Past Eight* revue which was the resident show at the Alhambra at that time. The performance, just for one night, was augmented by some of the English and American stars who would have been in the Royal Variety Performance. The royal party

Princess Alexandra and The Hon Angus Ogilvy entering the royal box at Jimmy Logan's Metropole Theatre, Glasgow, for a charity gala in aid of Stars Organisation for Spastics, April 1965. *Photograph courtesy of Jimmy Logan*

obviously enjoyed the show, even if it did overrun by half an hour, and before returning to Balmoral by train the Duke of Edinburgh commented that it had been well worth keeping British Rail waiting on this occasion.

The Queen's 1977 Jubilee celebrations in Scotland included visits to the theatre in Edinburgh and Glasgow, where a Royal Variety Performance was staged at the King's Theatre. This show included David Soul of *Starsky and Hutch* fame showing off his singing talents, Ronnie Corbett, Eric Sykes and Frankie Howerd in a kilt — 'Well, I'm half Scots,' he said. He was in fact the only touch of tartan in the show.

In 1965 Jimmy Logan, who had become one of Scotland's top entertainers, bought his own theatre in the city, the Metropole. Young Logan's boyhood ambitions of treading the boards had been fulfilled beyond his wildest dreams. Later he was also to play seasons at the London Palladium and have his own television series; more recently his televised performance of *Lauder* was a big success nationally.

After the performance at the Metropole, Princess Alexandra and The Hon Angus Ogilvy talking to Jimmy Logan and his sister, jazz singer Annie Ross, who also appeared in the show. *Photograph courtesy of Jimmy Logan*

Jimmy's Metropole Theatre played host to many stars, particularly in 1965 when he presented a Royal Gala Evening in aid of the 'Stars Organisation for the Spastics', SOS. Guest of honour was Her Royal Highness Princess Alexandra and her husband, the Honourable Angus Ogilvy. Logan had decorated the manager's office in Ogilvy tartan in honour of the occasion. It was a tiring night for the Scots entertainer, as he was not only appearing in the show but, as owner of the theatre, had to play host to the royal party. He had been planning the arrangements for several weeks before the event. Before the performance took place there was a delay while the florists finished decorating the Royal Box, only just giving the security authorities time to check the theatre, which normally takes an hour or so. Actually the royal car was held up in the traffic, and comedian Jack Radcliffe, who was keeping the audience amused until the royal party arrived, said to the audience, 'If they're much longer I'll have to show you my operation.' At the end of the show Logan said to the Princess in the manager's office that the company and staff were now ready for the customary presentation. The Princess remarked that Logan must be exhausted and told him to sit down first and have a drink: 'What shall I pour you?' she said. Jimmy had a Scotch while he got his breath back.

During the early fifties Logan was invited to give a concert at Wemyss Castle in Fife, where the hostess was Lady Victoria Wemyss, a godchild of Queen Victoria. Lady Wemyss's principal guests were Queen Elizabeth the Queen Mother and Princess Margaret. It was Jimmy's first appearance in the presence of royalty, and beforehand he was offered tea by Captain Wemyss in the dining-room where Mary Queen of Scots first met Lord Darnley.

This is almost where we came in as far as Scotland is concerned, but I'm sure there will be many more royal theatrical occasions in that lovely part of the world.

10

THAT'S ENTERTAINMENT

The Royal Variety Performance in London in 1958 was staged in the presence of Her Majesty the Queen and included at least one of the artistes she had seen in the Glasgow royal show earlier that year, Frankie Vaughan. Singer Vaughan has survived all the changes in entertainment during the past twenty years or more. His style and professionalism are such that I would recommend anybody learning the business to go and see Frank work. Max Bygraves compèred this show, and once again brought his polish to the performance, as did Roy Castle. I am not sure that Castle's talent is really appreciated in this country as it should be. He's a first-class musician, great dancer and light comedian of enormous charm. This was the show in which actor Bernard Bresslaw, another participant, was informed only a week before that he would be 'presented' after the performance, and would have to wear tails. Bresslaw didn't have a tail suit, and after scouring London without success (remember Bernard is not far short of six feet five) he was told that the Court tailors, Kilgour and French, could make him one in time. Now tailors such as these go into your background before taking an order just to make sure you're not a criminal or suchlike. The suit was duly made in time, but on the night Bresslaw was informed that he was to be presented in the costume he'd worn for his part in the performance. The tail suit in fact has never been worn because Bernard has put on some weight since then, so if anybody wants a very smart tall thin tail suit they know where they can find one.

There was no Royal Variety Performance in London in 1959, although Her Majesty did see the Crazy Gang in *Clown Jewels* at the Victoria Palace, and the musical *West Side Story*. However, there was a royal performance at the Palace Theatre Manchester. The theatre, recently given a face-lift to the tune of two million pounds, is a beautiful building and quite awe-inspiring to work in, as I found when I played there in the early sixties with the Shadows. The show at the Palace included the Hallé Orchestra, conducted by Sir John Barbirolli. Now Barbirolli was a great fan of music hall, and in his young days had played in the pit orchestra at the Wood Green Empire and elsewhere. At Manchester he had been given a comfortable dressing-room on his own. Also in the show, and sharing a dressing-room, were several comedians, including Dickie Henderson, Arthur Askey, Roy Castle, Jimmy Jewel and Ben Warris. At that time Jewel's and Warris's personal assistant was Alec Myles, now a writer and promoter, and Myles remembers Sir John Barbirolli knocking on the dressing-room door and asking if he could share the room with the comedy contingent. Asked why, when he had a room of his own, he said, 'I have always admired and had an affection for stand-up comedians, and I'd like to share this special night with you, all I ask is a nail on the wall to hang my coat.'

The sixties began with the legitimate theatre still playing to good business, but the variety theatre was beginning to lose its way. The two television channels obviously had something to do with this, but I will never accept that they were the real cause of variety's waning appeal with the general public. Apart from television, bingo was taking hold amongst the masses; as a nation we were being encouraged to buy our own houses, which meant buying new furniture and fittings. Everyone was becoming do-it-yourself conscious, and on top of that most people by now owned a car to take them away from the house at the weekend, the house that was taking more and more of their time and energy to keep in order. Holidays abroad were being advertised to such an extent that Spain was becoming a second Blackpool, complete with fish and chips.

The sixties were to be a decade of television and pop records. Elvis Presley had already made himself a folk hero, to be copied by our own new crop of pop stars, Cliff Richard, Tommy Steele, Marty Wilde, Billy Fury and suchlike. Only Cliff Richard and Tommy Steele were able to carry themselves into the future with any degree of success and become 'entertainers'. Theatre revue was given a completely new look by a group of undergraduates in a show called *Beyond the Fringe.* Peter Cook, Dudley Moore, Alan Bennett and Jonathan Miller have all carved out careers for themselves in different fields since then. Those four boys revolutionised revue just as the Goons had revolutionised radio comedy in the fifties.

Satire came to television in the form of a programme called *That Was The Week That Was,* and the whole cast made niches for themselves in varying degrees. David Frost, Roy Kinnear, Lance Percival, Millicent Martin and others are now well known personalities. Perhaps the most extraordinary rise to stardom since time began was the launching of a pop group from the Cavern Club in Liverpool. The Beatles smashed their way into the record charts and became living legends. I remember seeing the crowds outside the Civic Hall Portsmouth when they were appearing there, and it made the reception for Johnny Ray at the Palladium look like a Vicar's tea party! In 1963 the Beatles appeared in the Royal Variety Performance; that they were included in a royal show so early in their career is some indication of their enormous popularity and sudden rise to international stardom. John Lennon advised those in the cheap seats to clap; the rest could just rattle their jewellery.

There have been many star-studded royal shows, but the 1960 performance, at the Victoria Palace, the first one to be televised, included some of the biggest names, and was one of the most successful. The Crazy Gang made several appearances in items from their current production at the Palace, and even before the show started they were making the Queen laugh when they lined the stairs in the foyer dressed as Yeoman of the Guard. Charlie Drake was superb in a burlesque balloon dance routine. Robert Horton, the star of the American television serial *Wagon Train*, was in the cast. Liberace, who was determined to make up for his non-appearance in the 1956 royal show, which was cancelled due to the Suez crisis, brought a sparkle to the proceedings seldom seen before, and the line-up even had a seaside concert party in it, the Fol-de-Rols, for good measure.[1] Perhaps the biggest hit of the evening was Sammy Davis Junior. After the event the *Daily Sketch* newspaper said, 'Let's start by renaming last night's Royal Variety show at the Victoria Palace "The Sammy Davis Jr. Show". For, in eight electrifying minutes, this entertainer made the word "star" seem inadequate.'

Sammy had shown the audience what vaudeville and entertainment were all about. He sang, danced and joked his way through a routine which included some superb impressions, and as the reviews of the show had said, it was all done in eight minutes. Compère Bruce Forsyth led the slightly dazed Sammy Davis off-stage and then brought him back again, and again, for seven or eight curtain calls; it is generally not etiquette to take a call in a royal show, but the audience just would not let him go. He eventually went back upstairs to his dressing-room and the first person to congratulate him was the great Nat King Cole. However, the evening hadn't finished for Davis, as he, along with everyone else in the show, more than two hundred, were to join the Crazy Gang in choruses of their popular song 'Strolling'. The entire company, in tails and top hats, emerged from all directions on to the Victoria Palace stage for this vocal finale.

In the dressing-room beforehand Davis asked his manager where his suit was:

'Hanging right here, Sammy. All ready for you'. I ripped off my tux and jumped into the pants they'd sent. I didn't need to look at them in a mirror. I could feel the way they fit. 'They're like ten inches too big. This isn't my suit Murphy'. 'Yes it is Sammy. Look. It's got your name on it'. 'What are you going to do?' 'Do I have a choice? Give me a safety pin baby. We'll pull 'em up from behind so at least they'll stay on'. We pinned them. 'Well, it's not exactly my type of fit, but the tails'll cover it'. The Assistant Stage Manager called, 'two minutes please'. 'All right, lemme have the coat'. The sleeves dropped past where the shirt sleeves had gone. Murphy reached into a box and took out a black silk high hat. I put it on my head and it went plopppppppp! Over my ears. Completely over my ears. Only my nose stopped it. 'Come on Murphy. Give me *my* hat'. He was almost in tears. 'Sammy, this *is* your hat'. 'I don't believe it. I *won't* believe it. It's not true'. I sat down. 'I can't go on like this, that's all. It's impossible. I look like a Walt Disney character'. The door opened again. 'On stage for the Finale. On stage everybody'. I stuffed some Kleenex into the hatband and tried it again. At least it was resting on the top of my head. I stood in front of the mirror — baggy pants, gorilla-length sleeves, hat teetering on my head, the whole thing was like a Chaplin movie. We were singing 'Strolling' and everything was fine. The big finish to the show is when all the performers sing 'God Save the Queen'. Naturally when you sing this you remove your hat. The music strikes the first notes of 'God Save the Queen'. The audience is standing. I go for my hat with my right hand and as I move it from my side the sleeve falls, swoosh!, over my fingertips. I raise my arm, shaking my wrist to get my hand free, my fingers appear, and I can feel the hat. I get it off my head a few seconds behind everyone else and as I swing it down to my side the Kleenex flies out of the hat, sails over the Orchestra Pit into the audience, and hits a man in the face. It falls to his shoulder and he plucks it off with two fingers and drops it to the floor. I am so humiliated, so mortified that I'm praying I'll fall straight through the floor and never be seen or heard from again. We're coming to the last bars of 'God Save the Queen' and I'm thinking: how do I put the hat back on? I can't be the only one standing here holding his hat. The song is over. I put the hat on and it slides down over my ears and onto my nose. I try to tilt it back so maybe it'll catch on my forehead. I'm wrinkling my forehead trying to grip the hat with my eyebrows, but nothing helps. Only my mouth and chin are showing. All I can see is the inside of the hat, but I can hear the audience starting to fall apart. They're English and they're dignified and they've been trying to hold on, but there's a limit to everything and we'd passed it long ago. It would be poetic to say that as I fell asleep that night I also remembered myself as a child telling Mama 'someday I'm going to sing for the Queen of England'. Mama would surely have said 'yes, Sammy, if you want to sing for her you will'. But I didn't say it. As high as I had hoped, I never dreamed I'd have such a night.[2]

Another little incident worth recalling from that royal performance concerned Liberace, Robert Horton and that tail suit finale again. The two artistes were sharing a dressing-room and sent out an urgent SOS to say they couldn't get their tail suits on, and were becoming rather concerned, as the time was drawing near to join the rest of the company on stage. Agent Peter Prichard (you may remember him from the Mario Lanza incident) happened to be passing the dressing-room door and was asked to help. This he did, and had both Liberace and Robert Horton dressed in no time. It was just as well because Horton had broken out in an all-over rash from anxiety. Incidentally this was the only time that Liberace had appeared in anything but his own glittering wardrobe.

Comedian Norman Vaughan emerged during the early sixties when he took over as compère for ATV's *Sunday Night at the London Palladium*. Norman had been through all the various types of entertainment, from *Stars in Battledress*, concert party with Clarkson Rose's *Twinkle* and major variety bills. I have known Norman for nearly twenty years and I vividly remember meeting him the day he'd been told about the Palladium job.

Norman Vaughan with Bob Hope at the 1962 Royal Variety Performance. *Photograph courtesy Norman Vaughan*

HM The Queen accompanied by Earl Mountbatten of Burma arriving at the Theatre Royal Drury Lane for a gala performance of *Hello Dolly* in aid of the Historic Churches Preservation Trust, December 1965. *Photograph courtesy Press Association*

He came to see a broadcast I was doing and afterwards we went and had some lunch at Lyons in Coventry Street. When he confided the good news to me we celebrated with a tincture of the grape. I suppose nowadays one would open several bottles of champagne for an occasion like that, but we were both only just out of the half a pint of beer a week situation; that wine tasted like nectar, and to Norman I know it was a moment for the realisation of his dreams. He compèred the 1962 Royal Variety Performance, which also included Bob Hope. Norman's writer, Eric Merriman, had written him some lovely material for the occasion, including one of his linking spots which followed magician Johnny Hart. Hart used to, amongst other illusions, produce live doves out of handkerchiefs. The idea was for Norman Vaughan to follow him, doing a 'cod' handkerchief routine mimicking all the actions that Hart had done, and finally blowing his nose on the handkerchief as the pay-off. At the afternoon rehearsals before the show, Robert Nesbitt, the director, jumped up from the stalls and said, 'I'm sorry Norman, you can't blow your nose in front of Her Majesty.' There is absolutely no answer to that, is there?

Her Majesty the Queen's interest and attention to duty in patronising the royal charity performance must never be taken for granted. For instance, on one occasion she had to be up very early next morning for the State Opening of Parliament and her wishes to try and keep the show to time have always been adhered to as far as is humanly possible. As a result of the sort of world we live in today the sovereign's life is busier and fuller perhaps than any of her predecessors'.

One of the magic moments in a royal show was the occasion when Queen Elizabeth the Queen Mother attended a performance at the Prince of Wales Theatre. One of the stars was the elegant and charming Maurice Chevalier. Towards the end of his spot in the show Chevalier started to sing 'You must have been a Beautiful Baby', which continued 'You must have been a Wonderful Child,' etc. When he came to the last chorus he sang directly to the Queen Mother, finishing, 'yes, you must have been a beautiful baby, 'cos, Madam, look at you now.'

America's Jack Benny and George Burns joined forces in this show to recreate the famous duo of George Burns and Gracie Allen. Their weekly television programmes were a must for British viewers at one time, and George's familiar finishing line after Gracie had done one of her ridiculous and confusing monologues concerning in most cases her family became a show business catch-phrase. After a long look at the camera Burns would draw on his cigar and quietly say, 'Just say goodnight Gracie.' In the royal show at the Prince of Wales Jack Benny, in a costume resembling Gracie's, did a very creditable impersonation of the late comedienne, with George Burns playing himself, of course. This unique way of bringing the two comedians together was really only possible because Burns and Benny were lifelong friends. George Burns was a true vaudevillian, having been dancer, singer of sorts (his description) and superb raconteur. At a big dinner in America in his honour many well known personalities toasted Burns with the sort of humour he appreciates. One of the speakers was Ronald Reagan, a short while before he was elected President:

I just couldn't turn down this opportunity to say a few words about our man of the hour. George, Nancy my wife wanted me to tell you that you're her favourite singer, but then Harry Truman was her favourite piano player. If you're wondering why we're honouring this man tonight, who else do you know who was an actual eye-witness to most of the history of our country, the toast is George Burns.

Burns' reply was in the same vein and obviously underlined their affection for one another:

> I've known Ronnie Reagan for a long time. Every time I met him at a party we'd get up and sing a song together. Since then he became President of the Screen Actors Guild, Governor of California, and nominated for President of the United States. I can't understand it, where did I go wrong? I know I sing better than he does.[3]

In the sixties television situation comedy was gathering big audiences. *Hancock's Half Hour, Steptoe and Son, George and the Dragon, Till Death Us Do Part* and others were keeping people at home on certain nights of the week. Nearly all these shows made actors into personalities by virtue of their comic surroundings. The big variety spectaculars did not do justice to themselves on the small screen, but comedians, with or without stooges, still had their rightful place in the royal shows. Des O'Connor was compèring one of the performances and his 'stooge' on this occasion was Jack Douglas. Jack, before joining Des in many stage and television appearances, had been part of a double act, Baker and Douglas, in which the latter played the feed. With Des, Jack was in the character of Ippititimus, dressed in overalls, big boots, cap and steel-rimmed glasses, and sporting every now and again a nervous twitch. In this particular royal show there was little time to rehearse their piece, so a lot of it was ad lib on the night within the framework of their normal routine. On this occasion Jack Douglas came up through the audience and interrupted Des O'Connor on stage. Douglas was carrying a roll of red carpet under his arm and his first words to O'Connor were, 'Did I hear some Corgis barking?' Des asked, 'What are you doing with that roll of red carpet?' Jack's reply was 'I found it in the foyer, it's a disgrace, people have been wiping their feet on it.' Their spot was a huge success, as was O'Connor's compèring of the whole show. Jack Douglas was told he'd have to change into evening dress for the finale and the presentation to the Queen Mother, who was the principal royal guest that night. Des O'Connor said to the director that nobody would know who Jack was unless he was in the uniform of Ippititimus, and that if Jack couldn't come on in the finale as the character he'd portrayed in the show neither would he. The director relented and when Douglas was presented to the Queen Mother she said to him, 'Thank you for some marvellous laughter tonight, but may I say you're not the smartest man here this evening,' which dressed in the overalls, cap and boots etc., was the understatement

of the year. Incidentally, Jack Douglas suggested the title of this book. When I was touring with him in a play we had adjoining dressing-rooms at the Theatre Royal York, and one night I was telling him of my intentions to write this, but that I couldn't at that point think of a good title. Jack said, 'Why not "By Royal Command", as that is how most performers think of the honour of being included in a Royal Show?'

Several royal performers were now becoming regular Court Jesters and almost competing with the Crazy Gang for that title, although the 'Gang' perhaps were unique in their way. Max Bygraves, Norman Wisdom, Dickie Henderson, Bob Monkhouse, Morecambe and Wise, Harry Secombe and some singers — or perhaps entertainers is a better word for them — like Vera Lynn, Cliff Richard and Tommy Steele were familiar faces in the annual shows. A fairly new addition was Ken Dodd, although he had been very successful in the north of England for some time. He refused to come down to London until he thought he was ready to play the south, and the south was ready for him. When he did arrive, he was an instant success. In the real tradition of the music hall, with visual, outrageous audience participation comedy, Dodd chased his audience with a rapid stream of jokes nearly always bordering on the ridiculous rather like Billy Bennett did, with the eventual outcome that the audience capitulated in a state of exhaustion from the non-stop 'Doddy-osities' (that's my description, but could easily be his). His 'Diddymen' will surely go into the comic history books.

About this time BBC Television introduced colour into their recently established second channel, BBC2, although the royal performance was not shown in colour until 1970.

In 1968 the variety theatre mourned the death of one of its great clowns, the much loved Bud Flanagan. Bud, whose real name was Reuben Weintrop, began his career as a 12-year-old boy illusionist at the London Music Hall, and after various vaudeville tours of America and Australia joined the British Army and took part in concert party shows for the troops during the First World War. During these concerts he sang with the French star Mistinguett. During the early twenties he changed his name to Flanagan, and teamed up with an actor, Chesney Allen, in a revue. This partnership was to continue through the great hey-day of variety, with many seasons in the big revues in London, and it was the partnership of Flanagan and Allen, coupled with the Crazy Gang, that helped considerably in putting the Palladium on the map, as

Opposite: comedian Jack Douglas in his guise of Mr Ippititimus when he appeared with Des O'Connor in the 1966 Royal Variety Performance. *Photograph courtesy of J. Douglas*

HM The Queen with Princess Margaret and Lord Snowdon attending a performance at the Royal Opera House, Covent Garden, October 1968. *Photograph by Associated Newspapers*

well as the Victoria Palace. He had a great rapport with more than one generation of the Royal Family and it is generally recognised that Bud followed in the tradition of Dan Leno as the Court Jester. Flanagan received the OBE in 1960. He appeared in something like fifteen Royal Variety performances, a feat surpassed only by Max Bygraves, and several other royal gala occasions. A true vaudevillian had taken his last bow.

After a period out of the limelight, Frankie Howerd re-established himself in the sixties to his true position of merit. He had become a star very quickly with his regular appearances in the late forties in radio's *Variety Bandbox* and perhaps was not experienced enough to hold his new-found stardom so early in his career. Through his radio appearances he became a bill topper all over the country in variety, which was difficult for a young man. His first royal appearance was at a private party at Buckingham Palace in the presence of George VI and Queen Elizabeth. Howerd was a teetotaller then, but someone suggested that if he was nervous he should have a glass of port and brandy before going on. He got the drink and hid it behind a curtain in the dressing-room at the Palace, but Jimmy Edwards, who was also in the concert, found it, and drank it before Frankie could. On his way to this engagement he got hopelessly lost in the Palace courtyards as he had misinterpreted the policeman's directions and he went through one door after another, finally landing in the gardens. After the show he was presented to the King and Queen and the princesses (nearly falling over in his anxiety to bow in the correct manner). Her Majesty told him how delighted she was to meet him and how much she had enjoyed his performances on radio. In Howerd's own words:

> it was such a friendly homely atmosphere, and chatting with the Queen I got carried away and started telling her a long involved story. Her Majesty was very patient and in fact asked me to repeat the story to the King, but I thought I'd been boring enough.

Frankie, even now, feels he might be boring you with a story or anecdote; I suppose it's all part of the true 'funny man's' feeling of insecurity.

On the evening of a Royal Variety Performance, and Howerd has done several, he stays in his office in London until it is near the time for his appearance. He doesn't like being cooped up in a dressing-room through the long nervous period waiting to go on. He walks through the darkened streets going through his words. 'People must think I'm barmy,' he said. He gets permission to rehearse his act on stage at the Talk of the Town in the early morning a few days before the actual show, with just the cleaners for company. When he walks on to a stage he gives the impression he has just got off a bus and is going to have a chat with just one or two people over a cup of tea, discussing the latest gossip, dressed in a suit that you feel could do with a press, hair tousled and an opening gambit that is highly original: 'Now, er, listen, no wait, ooh I've had a shocking day, anyway, no don't laugh, titter ye not at the afflicted etc.' In a few seconds he has the audience snared in his web. This confidential approach to his comedy is the reason for his success on television. At one royal performance Lord Snowdon, who was accompanying the Queen Mother, laughed so much at Frankie that he almost fell off his chair. When the artistes were presented after the show Snowdon apologised to Howerd for laughing so loudly.

Michael Craig, Moira Anderson, Frankie Howerd and Peggy Mount enjoy a lighthearted moment with HM The Queen after the star-spangled gala at the Palladium in aid of the Army Benevolent Fund in April 1969. *Photograph courtesy of Associated Newspapers*

In one royal show in the sixties female impersonator Danny La Rue told Her Majesty the Queen that his performances were always tiring, as he generally made several quick changes during the course of the evening. Her Majesty said, 'I know what you mean, I do a few quick changes myself, you know.'

In the seventies the theatre in general was now fighting fierce competition from all three television channels, but still the annual royal performance was as popular as ever, with American stars still happy and honoured to be included.

Liza Minelli, the talented daughter of Judy Garland, told me she had her moment of panic in a royal show. She was singing her hit song 'Cabaret', and as she was obviously familiar with it she didn't have to think about her hand movements and gestures, they just came naturally every time she performed the song. In the show she started to play it as usual. She told me:

It didn't occur to me that during the part where I sing, 'I used to have this girlfriend known as Elsie, with whom I shared four sordid rooms in Chelsea. She wasn't what you'd call a blushing flower, as a matter of fact she rented by the hour. The day she died the neighbours came to snicker, well that's what comes from too much pills and liquor. But when I saw her laid out like a Queen. . .' at that moment I pointed my arm out — totally unaware that it was directed precisely at the Queen herself who was sitting in the Royal Box.

The year 1975 will live in my memory for a very long time. From early in 1974 I had been involved in the theatre in London at the Criterion in a play called *There Goes the Bride* and at the same time I was doing television and radio recordings for the *Dad's Army* series. While I was in the play I heard that *Dad's* was to go on stage in the form of a musical; the television version had already won the BAFTA award for the best television comedy series. We opened the stage musical of *Dad's Army* for a couple of weeks at the Forum Theatre Billingham before coming into the Shaftesbury Theatre in London, where we stayed for five months before going out on a six-month tour of the country. A few weeks after

HM The Queen, Princess Anne and the Duke of Edinburgh being received at the London Palladium for the Royal Variety Performance in November 1969. *Photograph courtesy of Press Association*

The BAFTA award-winning original cast of *Dad's Army*, 1972. Left to right, standing: John Laurie, David Croft (producer), Arnold Ridley, the author, James Beck, Jimmy Perry (writer), Ian Lavender. Sitting: left to right, John Le Mesurier, Arthur Lowe and Clive Dunn. *Photograph courtesy of BBC*

we had opened we were asked to stay on stage one night after the finale, as the management had an announcement to make. It was to tell us that we had been invited to take part in the Royal Variety Performance in the presence of the Queen and Duke of Edinburgh at the Palladium in November. I can tell you that there was just a little celebrating by the cast that night!

When the weekend arrived for the royal show we had to use the Shaftesbury as our base and we would be shuttled backwards and forwards to the Palladium by coach for rehearsals. Most of Sunday and Monday we went back and forth along Oxford Street with packs of sandwiches and flasks of coffee (oh the glamour of it all). There had been a number of bomb scares in the West End that autumn, and we had had a couple at the Shaftesbury when the performance had to be halted while the theatre was searched. At the Palladium the security was very tight. We were continually being searched and given identity papers, but no one minded, as we were all glad that so much trouble was being taken for our safety. The afternoon prior to the performance was, as usual, taken up with the dress rehearsal and the last-minute details. Bruce Forsyth, who was compèring the show, was working like a beaver getting all his linking material together and talking with the artistes he would be introducing. Telly Savalas (Kojak) was carefully rehearsing part of his Las Vegas cabaret routine which he would be doing in the show. Vera Lynn was sitting in the stalls bar drinking a cup of coffee with her husband and pretty daughter. This lovely lady must have had in her life a greater following in this country than perhaps any other singer. 'Forces Sweetheart' in the Second World War, she toured all the battle fronts, and today she still has a warm and magnetic voice. Something made me laugh just before the finale of the show, which I'm sure would have made Vera giggle if she'd known about it. Harry Secombe, who had not cancelled the performance of his show currently at the Prince of Wales Theatre, was to finish this royal performance with Vera Lynn and the Welsh Choir. Harry came in hotfoot from his theatre, having rehearsed his royal piece in the afternoon, ready to join Vera, who was already on stage. Harry stood in the wings for a moment and called out, 'Go on girl, you're doing fine — get your knickers off.' Harry has to let off steam, but — here we are on this special occasion in the presence of our sovereign, and Harry has to let loose as only he can. Mind you, even if anybody had heard it, other than those around him, it is difficult to imagine him offending anyone.

Charles Aznavour was a little late for rehearsals in the afternoon, having been delayed at the airport in Paris. Count Basie and his Orchestra seemed to be everywhere; Basie, a quiet man, was very popular with the British contingent, as was Telly Savalas. All this time Robert Nesbitt was directing, organising and persuading all the artistes to follow the instructions that he had worked out long before we had got to the Palladium that weekend.

After rehearsals we were all dispersed to different buildings around the Palladium to await our call to go over to the theatre just before the show was due to start. The Count Basie Orchestra were hidden at the top of Liberty's store in Regent Street, while 'Dad's Army' and the 'Billy' company from Drury Lane were holed up in the dining-room of a nearby pub. I don't know where the Kwa Zulu African dance company and the Welsh Rhos Male Voice Choir were housed, but I believe they were all together in some large establishment near at hand. It must have been an interesting situation. We moved into the Palladium about fifteen minutes before curtain up and eventually heard the tannoy announcement that Her Majesty and the Duke had arrived in the theatre. The excitement was growing fast, but as usual Arthur Lowe was having his

The cast of *Dad's Army* being presented to HM The Queen and the Duke of Edinburgh after the 1975 Royal Variety Performance at the London Palladium. Left to right: HRH The Duke of Edinburgh, Lord Delfont, the author, HM The Queen, Ian Lavender, Arnold Ridley, Clive Dunn, John Le Mesurier and Arthur Lowe. The lady next to Arthur Lowe is impressionist Janet Brown. *Photograph by Doug McKenzie, PPS*

Scroll presented to the author commemorating his appearance in the 1975 Royal Variety Performance. *Photograph courtesy of Bill Pertwee*

customary pre-show nap accompanied by just a little snoring. We heard the National Anthem and then Bruce Forsyth's first spot which was obviously getting them going, as we say. Soon it was our turn to move on to the stage and wait behind the curtain as Bruce and Michael Crawford did a double piece out front, and then the announcement came: 'Ladies and Gentlemen, Dad's Army'. The curtain went up and we were momentarily blinded by the front spots as we went into the 'Floral Dance' routine we had previously done in the television series and were currently featuring in our Shaftesbury show.

In the foyer afterwards, during the presentation of the cast to the Queen and Prince Philip, I noticed that hardly anyone spoke to the Queen, so when she got to me I shook hands as is customary and then said, 'Did you enjoy it Ma'am?' The Queen said, 'Very much thank you, it was nice to see you on stage after having seen you on television.' The Duke of Edinburgh was very relaxed and said he'd enjoyed our piece. Ronnie Dukes, of Dukes and Lee, who performed a very fast dance in their variety act, was standing quite near me and the Duke of Edinburgh said to Ronnie, 'You're fast on your feet, yet you are so small and your legs are little.' Ronnie replied, 'Well, Sir, I was as tall as you when I started dancing.'

It is very, very seldom that an artiste is asked to add to his rehearsed piece at one of these performances — normally they are asked to cut, but when the late Bill Haley was included in 1979 he was such a hit at rehearsals with his 'Rock Around the Clock' that he was asked to include 'See you Later, Alligator'. Her Majesty the Queen was seen to be thoroughly enjoying his spot and afterwards at the presentation she said to Haley, 'You know we grew up with you.' Well, who didn't?

Nineteen seventy-seven was the year of Her Majesty the Queen's Silver Jubilee and obviously this called for something special in the way of theatrical celebration. A Royal Gala Performance was arranged at the Palladium for the benefit of several charities, including the EABF. It had been arranged by Lord Delfont and his brother Lord Grade that the television version would be sold to America. Reg Swinson, the EABF Secretary, thought it might be a good idea to invite Lord Delfont and Lord Grade's mother Mrs Winogradsky to present the bouquet to Her Majesty in the foyer on her arrival. Mrs Winogradsky asked Swinson what she should say to the Queen. Swinson said, 'Just say good evening.' The old lady said, 'But supposing the Queen asks me about my boys?' Just like a mum. She was always terribly proud of her three sons, Bernard, Lew and Leslie.

In addition to the annual Royal Variety Performance the Queen and her family, during the past twenty years particularly, have spent whole evenings attending hundreds of gala occasions from Scotland to Jersey, Surrey to Yorkshire, London to Newcastle, Eastbourne to Norwich, in support of many, many charities. They could be excused, with all the other duties they have to attend to, for only spending a quick half-hour at a function, saying, 'Hello, good evening — thanks for raising the money' and then off home. Just as the Royal Family use their time and energies in earning money for this country through their estate businesses and maintaining our pageantry for the enormous tourist trade we have come to rely on, so they are also willing participants, when time allows, in the business of raising money for charity. A gentleman called Billy Marsh has been responsible for arranging a great many of these gala performances all over the country. Marsh has also long been involved in the organising of the Royal Variety performances with Lord Delfont and Louis Benjamin, and his vast experience is much valued. Billy Marsh began his career as an agent with Lord Delfont many years ago and is now head of London Management, a representation agency that has in its time been responsible for managing a tremendous number of top stage and screen performers, and I know he is held in high esteem by the artistes he represents.

In one charity performance at the Palladium in aid of the Heart

Actress Mollie Sugden and actor William Moore being presented to HM The Queen after a Silver Jubilee Gala Performance at the Windsor big top, 1977. In the background are 'Dame Edna' (Barry Humphreys) and Leo Sayer. *By courtesy of W. Moore. Photograph Doug McKenzie, PPS*

Foundation which the Queen Mother was attending, Marsh had arranged for Morecambe and Wise to star in the show, but they had a recording to do at the television studios first. The 'boys' were held up for a while, and in the interval the Queen Mother asked, 'Have Eric and Ernie arrived yet?' Marsh said, 'No, but they won't be long I'm sure, let's have a glass of champagne and we'll delay the start of the second half a little longer.' The boys arrived and entertained the Queen Mother and the rest of the audience in true Eric and Ernie style.

In the early fifties Prince Philip attended a gala concert at the London Coliseum in aid of the National Playing Fields Association. The show included a troupe of 40 girls, 20 currently at the Adelphi Theatre and 20 from the Victoria Palace, all amalgamated together for this one performance. As a result of the Duke's attendance a number of American stars agreed to appear, including Frank Sinatra, Orson Welles, Tony Curtis and Janet Leigh. The charity did extremely well that night.

At one gala evening at a Watford night club attended by Princess Margaret, the cabaret was compèred by David Frost, an old friend of the organiser Richard Afton. When Frost arrived for the pre-show cocktail party he was rewarded with a big hug from Princess Margaret and a personal thank-you for arranging his busy schedule to include the show. This was the first time the musical act of Dukes and Lee had appeared at a royal show, and they were a big hit with the audience. Princess Margaret got to her feet calling for more and joining in the ovation for these popular artistes.

On another occasion Richard Afton asked David Frost whether he would host a royal gala evening at a club at Stoke-on-Trent. Frost at that time had a heavy list of engagements in America, but told Afton that he would try to rearrange his dates so that he could do it, which he did. He flew to London, had a helicopter waiting at Heathrow to fly him to Stoke, and the next morning did the journey in reverse back to the States — all at his own expense.

A gala performance was arranged by Afton at a night club in Luton which was to be attended by the Duke of Edinburgh. He had sent a message by his equerry to say that he wished to leave immediately after the dinner and cabaret. Afton arranged for the Duke's car to be ready on time, and told His Royal Highness that a VIP room was at his disposal at one end of the club. The big bar had been cordoned off for the cabaret artistes to relax in. Before leaving, the Duke asked if he could have a beer. This was brought to him and then he enquired whether the artistes could join him in the VIP room. Afton told him that it was really too small to accommodate them all, so the Duke said, 'Well, if they can't come to us, let us go to them.' This he did, and almost immediately got into a friendly argument with Les Dawson, who had taken part in the cabaret, about the best way to cook black pudding. Dawson said it should be boiled, split down the middle, and served with butter. The Duke said he liked it fried — and that was the proper way to cook it. It is obvious that gala performances not only raise a lot of money for charity but also raise their quota of fun for the entertainers and those they are entertaining, including members of the Royal Family.

Notes

1. More details on the Fol-de-Rols can be found in *Pertwee's Promenades and Pierrots*, by Bill Pertwee (Westbridge Books, a division of David & Charles, 1979).
2. With Sammy Davis Jr.'s permission, from his autobiography, *Yes I Can* (Cassell, 1965).
3. George Burns, *Third Time Around* (W. H. Allen, 1980).

11

'FINALE'

It was in 1978 that Lord Delfont bowed out of the hot seat as far as presenting the annual Royal Variety Performance was concerned. This quiet man, whose charm and tact had steered the annual show through 21 years of laughter, tears and nervous tensions, could hardly have achieved more in his position as overall producer during a period when fashions in entertainment were changing so rapidly. Was it all worthwhile for him? 'After the event it always was,' he told me. As the years went on, Lord Delfont felt more and more nervous each time the big night arrived, and who could blame him? To produce a show of that magnitude takes a lot of courage in the first place, because you know you are never going to please everyone. With his director Robert Nesbitt, who is without doubt one of the greatest stage directors in this country, Delfont for just one night of the year brought together many talents and moulded the natural temperaments of great artistes into a whole for presentation to the sovereign. There have been disappointments. Elvis Presley was invited, but declined, though he did send a substantial cheque to swell the charitable funds. Elton John thought he could have done better and sent a donation after the event, perhaps easing his own disappointment. There have been moments of elation too for Lord Delfont — for instance at the 1978 royal show, when he was given a huge personal reception from artistes, audience and the Royal Box in gratitude for the magnificent job he had done for the event since he took charge.

If you know something of Lord Delfont's background, you may wonder how he ever had time for his immense task. They always say, however, that if you want anything done well, go to the busiest man in the village. Delfont has always been the busiest man in the village of show business. His achievements have encompassed every area of the theatre. He began his career as a dancer, later became a successful artistes' agent and then in the early forties moved into production. He has assumed management of many theatres during the past forty years, including the St Martin's, the Saville, the Casino (now the King Edward Theatre), the Prince of Wales and the Shaftesbury. He converted the London Hippodrome into the Talk of the Town restaurant in the late fifties; this is now one of the most successful show places in Europe. He still presents many spectacular revues in the major seaside resorts and elsewhere. His latest West End theatrical venture took place at the Theatre Royal Drury Lane. In more recent years he has become the Chairman and Managing Director of the EMI film and theatre corporation in this country. When he took over the responsibility of presenting the Royal Variety performances from the then Palladium boss Val Parnell, Delfont was already heavily involved in an enormous amount of show business activities and charitable organisations. He is a past President of the Variety Club of Great Britain and is also a Life President of the Entertainment Artistes Benevolent Fund.

When Delfont began putting the annual royal shows together he knew that it was imperative to keep the production alive and fresh because the Entertainment Artistes Benevolent Fund and Brinsworth House are reliant on this event for the bulk of their income.

Brinsworth House at Twickenham is a most comfortable rest home with a relaxed and friendly atmosphere. The Royal Family has always taken a great interest in Brinsworth and the first extension to the house was opened in 1919 by Princess Louis, Duchess of Argyll. A further extension was opened in 1961 by Princess Alexandra. The new and very modern wing was opened by Queen Elizabeth the Queen Mother in 1976, a memorable occasion for the residents. It would be very remiss of me if I didn't mention Denville Hall at Northwood, an equally comfortable home for actors and actresses which is also very welcoming. A third small residence which is aided by theatre charities is Evelyn Norris House at Worthing. It is heartening to know that performers from all the entertainment media are able to help their own, just as they are happy to spend a deal of their time in helping to raise money for practically every other charity in the country.

The EABF, so ably run by its Secretary Reg Swinson and his secretary, Mary Jane Burcher, provides benevolence for many retired performers who are living on their own or who are sick and in need of extra comfort. Over the years the EABF has received the support and assistance of the Grand Order of Water Rats, of which Lord Delfont is one of their Companion Rats, along with Prince Philip, Prince Charles, Billy Marsh and Bobby Butlin, the son of the late holiday camp king Sir William Butlin, who did such an enormous amount for charitable causes when he was alive. The Water Rats who have appeared in royal performances are far too numerous to mention, but just a few past King Rats of the order are Dan Leno, Harry Tate, Will Hay, Georgie Wood, Robb Wilton, Bud Flanagan, Ted Ray, Ben Warris, Tommy Trinder, Charlie Chester, Frankie Vaughan, David Nixon and boxer Henry Cooper. The organisa-

Gala evening given by the Grand Order of Water Rats to one of their companions —
HRH The Duke of Edinburgh, March 1980. Left to right: Louis Benjamin, William
Foux, Billy Marsh, Chas McDevitt, HRH The Duke of Edinburgh, Henry Cooper, the
author, David Berglas, Alan Crooks (secretary of the Water Rats), Harry Seltzer, Al
French, John Street and Eddie Reindeer. *Photograph Doug McKenzie, PPS*

tion numbers only 200 at any one time throughout the world, and some
past 'Rats' who I know have been very proud of their association include
Laurel and Hardy, Charlie Chaplin, Ben Lyon and Peter Sellers.
Originally the Order of Water Rats was formed by a small group of performers who had been presented with a pony which they decided to race,
donating any monies they might win to their less fortunate comrades in
show business. On the day of the first race it was raining heavily and one
of the group observed that the pony 'looked like a drowned water rat'.
On the spur of the moment the group decided to call the pony 'Water
Rat' and themselves 'The Rats'. The small acorn grew into the respected
organisation that today is known as the GOWR. It is in being to help
their members or their families who are in need and to assist the EABF
and other charities such as the National Playing Fields Association,

HM Queen Elizabeth The Queen Mother meeting some of the stars after the 1980 Royal Variety Performance. Left to right: the producer Louis Benjamin, HM The Queen Mother, American stars Lillian Gish, Danny Kaye, Larry Hagman (J. R. of *Dallas*), Mary Martin (Hagman's mother), and British comedian Bruce Forsyth. *Photograph Doug McKenzie, PPS*

Cancer Research, etc. where they can. This small band of entertainers has achieved miracles over the years in raising funds, and I know they are grateful to the many members of the public who in turn help their efforts.

As far as the Royal Variety Performance was concerned, who was to take over from Lord Delfont? The task fell to Louis Benjamin, a small, neat man already Vice-Chairman and Managing Director of Moss Empires, a position to which he had risen from office boy with Moss's. He obviously knew the problems involved in presenting the annual show, but when you meet him you realise that he actually enjoys having that responsibility. He did have, for his first show in 1979 in the presence of Her Majesty the Queen, the moral support of Lord Delfont, who was on hand to help if needed, but Louis Benjamin had to do it his way, not because he wanted to try to be different for the sake of it, or prove he didn't want to call on anybody's past experience — no, it was just that as an individualist it came quite naturally to him to bring his own ideas to the production. I spent two days with the rehearsals for the 1980 Royal Variety Performance at the Palladium and those two days for Benjamin were the culmination of months of planning: meetings with Norman Maen, his director, assistant director Lionel Blair, and Yvonne Littlewood, who would be in charge of the television presentation which in 1980 was the responsibility of the BBC; talks with Reg Swinson, the Secretary of the EABF, to discuss programme details; hotel bookings for the weekend of the show for overseas performers. Hotels must naturally be of a high standard, as some artistes, having flown thousands of miles, will need all the rest they can get so that they are in the best frame of mind to cope with the hectic and nerve-racking 48-hour period of rehearsals and the performance itself. It is sometimes necessary for a whole production at some theatre or other to close on the Monday night if its star or stars are irreplaceable for that one evening. If this is the case, then compensation to the management for loss of box-office returns has to be considered. Hire cars have to be organised to take artistes backwards and forwards to their hotels or homes if they are living in London. The tight schedule of the whole weekend has to be adhered to: you can't chance someone not being able to park if they use their own transport, and anyway the problems of driving in the West End would be an added burden to them. Programme sellers and stewards have to be organised, and front-of-house staff thoroughly disciplined so that from the moment of the arrival of the royal party everything goes like clockwork. Security has to be discussed with the royal household and the police, and special security staff engaged for the night. Extra helpers have to be on hand during rehearsals to take care of the performers when they arrive, get them coffee, show them to their dressing-rooms, arrange the lunch schedule and make them feel generally as comfortable and relaxed as possible.

All this and more has to be discussed. Then there are the meetings which go on all through the year with the production group itself: the format of the show, the type of artistes that the Royal Family like to see, the long-distance telephone calls to Hollywood or wherever concerning the American contingent who will appear, the amount of time they are asked to do in the show (sometimes not always agreeable to the artistes concerned, who are, after all, giving their services for nothing) and airline bookings, which have to be made in good time. The British contingent, who will form the bulk of the show, have to be well catered for. With an audience in excess of twenty million watching the show on television, a performer wants to be seen to best advantage. The huge orchestra and the various artistes' conductors have to be consulted. The television company who will cover the event have to be in on the early meetings to discuss the best positions for their cameras, for there will be many of them in the auditorium, in the foyer and outside the theatre. Space must be found for the production control vehicles, lighting, sound, wardrobe, etc. in streets nearby. Nowadays the show has to cater for three audiences — the Royal Family, the paying customers in the theatre and the television audience at home. There has to be tremendous and willing co-operation between the stage director and his staff and the television director. This must all be thrashed out before the weekend of the show, because there is no time once the rehearsals begin at the theatre. The resident stage staff have to be in on every aspect of the operation, for scenery may have to be taken down and stored for the weekend and artistes' dressing-rooms have to be cleared to accommodate up to perhaps ten performers who will be sharing for this short period.

All this has to be the overall responsibility of one man sitting in his office high above Leicester Square, who has, in addition, to supervise the normal everyday running of Moss Empires, which includes the London Palladium. So when Louis Benjamin arrives at the theatre on Sunday morning for the first on-stage rehearsals he hopes he has covered all the eventualities, all the possible snags that could arise. Sitting with him in the auditorium I was amazed at Benjamin's cool. Every now and again he consulted with Norman Maen and Yvonne Littlewood, the television director, over some point in the staging, and I can't remember hearing a raised voice from the production team. The Sunday rehearsals are concentrated on seeing that the various sets all work and can be got on and off in the most practical way. The music, which has been previously orchestrated, is gone through, and any alteration required attended to on the spot, in this case by the overall MD, Ronnie Hazelhurst, and his orchestrator. The television camera angles and the lighting and sound are thoroughly rehearsed, and if you saw the sheer amount of lighting and sound equipment you would wonder just how it all comes together, but it does.

On the actual day, Monday, the Palladium starts to fill up with all the personalities who will take part. Mary Jane Burcher, Reg Swinson and Louis Benjamin's secretary welcome them all as they come in. Roy Hudd, who will be doing an impression of Max Miller, laughs nervously and talks a lot about the various artistes he is sharing the room with, all mates; apparently a non-stop barrage of gags from Tommy Trinder has been keeping them all amused. Billy Dainty walks around with a slightly bemused look — he will be impersonating Bud Flanagan with the original Chesney Allen, now in his eighty-sixth year but still looking exactly as he did when he partnered Bud all those years ago. Sandy Powell, with his wife Kay, sits quietly in the stalls reminiscing about his first royal appearance 45 years ago.

The overture having been rehearsed, it is the moment for Joe Loss to bounce on to the stage to conduct 'In the Mood', and how he sets us alight. When he's finished everyone in the theatre applauds this extremely fit and lively band leader who is celebrating fifty years in the business. This is certainly going to be a great start to the show. Joe and his orchestra have played at various royal functions, including Her Majesty the Queen's 50th birthday party at Windsor Castle in 1976. Joe was at the time engaged with his band on a *QE2* cruise and he told me that when the directors of Cunard heard he had been asked to play at the birthday celebrations, they made arrangements for him to leave the ship in the Middle East and fly home. After the party he flew straight back again and joined the cruise at Naples. Next come the Norman Maen dancers with Lionel Blair and the delightful Una Stubbs. Una has done so much good work in her career and just recently it has all paid off with the recognition of her 'Aunt Sally' character in the television series *Worzel Gummidge*. During the rehearsals various reporters, columnists and radio and television commentators are talking to artistes in odd corners of the auditorium. Next comes the neat and tidy Arthur Askey performing his 'Bee' song with the utmost economy. He's 80 years old and still superb. This is followed by a line-up of stars, all of them previous royal performers, in a nostalgic couple of choruses of 'Strolling' led by Chesney Allen, then young Paul Squires giving a performance of vitality and assurance normally associated with someone more experienced. Paul had been through his entire act for Louis Benjamin several days earlier on the Palladium stage, and had also spent a day or two walking about the empty auditorium getting the feel of its atmosphere. Bruce Forsyth makes his entrance on roller skates, and immediately starts gagging with the orchestra. Petite singer Sheena Easton, along with Paul Squires making her royal début, handles the whole situation with great ease and professionalism. Rowan Atkinson almost shambles on, oblivious to the quiet chatter that is part of this whole day. Gradually the talk stops, as first the black contingent of Grace Kennedy, Aretha Franklin and their musicians start to laugh at this young man, followed by many more of us watching. One or two of the older pros are not sure. It's a bit different, this piece of Rowan's, he's portraying a political after-dinner speaker; I hear someone say, 'Where are the jokes?' Rowan's act isn't like that, and I'm certain he's going to be a hit with Prince Charles, who will be accompanying Queen Elizabeth the Queen Mother to the show. Harry

Worth can't be found; Billy Dainty says, 'He's thrown in the towel,' somebody else says, 'He's left his vent doll on the bus,' another says, 'He's a bloody nuisance, keeping us waiting, we'll not have time for a proper lunch break.' The director, Norman Maen, does enquire if anybody has seen Harry. Harry appears in a slightly confused state and says he didn't get a call to say he was wanted. Norman Maen just says, 'Thank you, Harry, when you're ready,' and Harry Worth plunges into the 'vent' act that earned him a very good living on the halls before he went into television situation comedy.

Richard Afton, ex-BBC television producer, is sitting next to me and we're joined by Arthur Askey and Roy Hudd. Roy tells me about the time he appeared in a royal gala with Richard Burton. Roy's feed Michael Harvey was standing next to Burton in the line-up and Burton said to him, 'Have you seen my wife anywhere?' to which Harvey replied, 'No, what does she look like?' Burton was then married to Elizabeth Taylor. Roy Hudd says, 'Harvey always was absent minded.'

Charlie Drake is standing at the back of the stalls drinking a cup of coffee and looks a lonely figure. We chat about the time he and I were both starting in the business and used to go down to the Forces Nuffield Centre at Charing Cross and do our acts for the price of a cup of coffee and a sandwich in the hope of being discovered by one of the many agents who frequented the little theatre every week. Charlie Drake has done some remarkably fine work since those days. The florists are still working in the Royal Box, decorating it with garlands of flowers. Suddenly there's a cry of joy from Lionel Blair — Sammy Davis has arrived. They both hug one another and Lionel introduces Sammy to me, as he knows I would like a first-hand account of Sammy's triumph in the 1960 royal performance. Sammy chats with me, moves up on to the stage to the delight of everyone in the theatre, and starts his routine. Very quickly he's got us all in the palm of his hand, just as he will the audience when it comes to the show.

I go and talk to Victor Borge, who has had us all rocking with laughter at his ad libs and the set routine he's going to do at night. He tells me that he was asked to do a concert a few years ago at Luton Hoo for Lady Zia Wernher and was told that Her Majesty the Queen would be present. When Borge arrived at the beautiful house he was asked quite seriously by Lady Wernher whether her dog could assist him in his piano act because apparently it was a bit of a canine wonder on the keyboard. Borge declined, saying he had a set routine. Half-way through his act in the evening the door opened and the dog walked in, sat near Borge and, when he had finished one particular piece, leapt on to the piano, dashed up and down the keys and left the room just as quietly as it had entered.

HRH Prince Charles who accompanied The Queen Mother to the 1980 Royal Variety Performance meets some of the stars after the show. Left to right: Victor Borge, Borge's assistant, Henry Mancini, Lord Delfont and His Royal Highness. *Photograph Doug McKenzie, PPS*

Tommy Trinder joins us while singer Peggy Lee is rehearsing her piece; what a good musician she is, every note of music is savoured and used to great effect. Tommy Trinder tells me a nice story about 'Monsewer' Eddie Gray, who was one of the great characters of the business and was a part of the Crazy Gang for many years. In the line-up for presentation after one royal performance Trinder was standing next to Gray waiting for the Queen Mother, then the Queen, to pass along the line. The Queen spoke to Maurice Chevalier in fluent French for several minutes and then came to Eddie Gray. Now part of Eddie's comedy juggling routine involved using a lot of cod French, and when he was presented to the Queen on this occasion he said to her, 'Vous can parly Francais Avec with me now if you want to Madame.' The Queen replied, 'I'm sorry, Mr Gray, I don't speak your kind of French.' Eddie Gray said, 'What a turn up for the book Mam.' Only Gray could get away with that sort of nonsense. Henry Mancini starts going through his piano playing quietly, and just as we are relaxing with Mancini's music, in comes Danny Kaye, tanned and wearing a blue denim casual suit, to be greeted by Benjamin and everyone else like an old friend. Danny, of course, is a seasoned campaigner at the Palladium. After the greetings he walks round the auditorium, absorbing all the familiar features of the theatre, then climbs on to the stage to speak to the orchestra and some of the artistes there. Benjamin meanwhile tells me there might be a surprise or two for the performance. I was right on one guess, that Larry Hagman's mother Mary Martin would be one of the surprises, but I hadn't thought about James Cagney and Pat O'Brien. The finale is next to be rehearsed and can you imagine what a work of art it is to get everyone on to that stage in a neat and tidy order — dancers, singers, musicians and all the principal artistes — ready for the National Anthem? One person has not yet rehearsed; in fact, he's only just arrived in the theatre under tight security — 'J.R.' (Larry Hagman). This is the moment for the tea break and the theatre to be cleared of unnecessary bodies. As we start to leave I notice Angela Rippon, who is to introduce the television transmission, quietly making notes on a clipboard.

Louis Benjamin will shortly be going home to change and prepare himself for the performance that will be the culmination of a year's planning. What are his thoughts at that point? 'It is too late now to think of what I should have done, I should have already done everything humanly possible to ensure there are no snags.' He is going to get back to the theatre in good time so that he can make sure that his front-of-house staff are quite happy about their role in the event. He knows them all personally of course, from John Avery, the manager, to every member of the Palladium personnel. Naturally tensions grow as the time draws near for the royal arrival. Just a few miles away the Queen Mother and Prince Charles prepare for their evening of entertainment, an evening that without their attendance would result in the EABF being many thousands of pounds worse off.

In the dressing-rooms the nervous apprehension of what is basically a first night is beginning to build up, but in this case there will be no second bite of the cherry. Someone says, 'It's no use, I'll have to go to the loo again.' There's the sound of leather being banged on concrete as another cigarette is stamped on the floor.

Some will make a name for themselves and be hailed overnight as stars; others will not do so well, but everyone will be in there trying. Over the tannoy comes the message that the royal party has arrived, and after some presentations in the theatre foyer the Queen Mother and her grandson will move into the Royal Box, the National Anthem will be played and the first artistes in the show will move down to the side of the stage. The curtains open, the stage is ablaze with light that blinds you as you walk on, and then comes the first burst of applause for the performance as Gordon Jackson walks slowly down to the footlights to deliver the prologue accompanied by a solo piper and drummer. The 1980 Royal Variety Performance has begun. A rather special performance because this one is in celebration of the 80th birthday of the Queen Mother — a lady much loved and respected by members of the theatrical profession.

When it's all over the talk and chatter are non-stop, but now it's all uninhibited — 'What a thrill to see Cagney and O'Brien, they kept their appearance quiet, didn't they?' — 'Rowan Atkinson did well, didn't he?' — 'I'll bet the Queen Mother was pleased to see Stanley Holloway, he's marvellous for 90 plus, isn't he?' — 'Sammy Davis was great as usual' — 'What about Larry Hagman forgetting the words of his song; wasn't his Mum, Mary Martin, smashing?' 'I hear Hagman wants his dry [mistake] to be kept in the television transmission when it goes out,

At the same performance, HM The Queen Mother talks to Sammy Davis Junior. Next to Davis is Arthur Askey. Louis Benjamin, far right, looks on in approval. *Photograph Doug McKenzie, PPS*

it just shows you what a nice human bloke the man is, different from the character he plays in Dallas.'

And now it's the presentation; the Queen Mother and Prince Charles, accompanied by Benjamin and Lord Delfont in his position of Life President of the EABF, are making their way along the line of artistes, thanking each one in turn for their generosity and co-operation in making this great night of entertainment possible. Prince Charles has stopped to talk to Ben Warris and some of the other great veterans of variety. The conversation gets round to dancing (nearly every pro in the hey-day of vaudeville could dance a step or two) and Prince Charles says that he would like to have been able to tap-dance but could never master it. Ben Warris tells the Prince that when he was working in variety with

Louis Benjamin greeting HRH Princess Margaret when she arrived for the first Children's Royal Variety Performance ever staged, London Palladium, March 1981.

Lord Delfont in their early days, 'Bernie' (Lord Bernard Delfont) was a great exponent of the art. Delfont then goes into a short soft shoe shuffle. A few bars of 'Bye, Bye Blues' and the master shows that once a pro always a pro. I think the same could be said of Ben Warris, who is without doubt one of the most knowledgeable men in the business; his memories, crystal clear, go back over sixty years. After saying his thanks to the royal party for gracing the occasion and seeing them safely on their way home, Louis Benjamin makes sure that he has thanked everyone in the theatre for their great help during a long and very busy weekend.

Tomorrow is another day for Benjamin, and he will be back in his office in the morning where normal business will be resumed, plus of course some time spent in writing personal thank-you letters. An hour or so will be put aside to start thinking about the 1981 Royal Variety Performance and his new baby, the Children's Royal Show at the Palladium in aid of children's charities, to be attended by Princess Margaret, an event he hopes will happen every year. While there are people like Benjamin and his predecessors, and all the hundreds of performers, variety acts, circus artistes, pop stars, sportsmen, actors and actresses from television and the theatre from all over the world ready to give their time and energy to raising money, and while we have a Royal Family who continue to play their star role in productions up and down the country, large and small, then I know we shall have a theatre ready to play their part by royal command.

ACKNOWLEDGEMENTS

Acknowledgements for a book of this kind can give you nightmares, because to leave anyone out would be unforgivable. I am extremely grateful for all the help, large or small, which has been so willingly given.

To Lord Delfont, for agreeing to write the Foreword, I extend a special thanks; Anne Wall, assistant Press Secretary to HM the Queen, who furnished me with some valuable details; Louis Benjamin and the Press Office of Moss Empires, whose co-operation was most gratifying; Max Bygraves for his precise and detailed contribution; Ronnie Tate, who kindly lent me pictures and scripts belonging to his father, Harry Tate; Billy Marsh; George Bartram for the information on Joe Loss and Dukes and Lee; Reg Swinson; Audrey Leno, for the loan of the Dan Leno illustrations; Jimmy Logan for his contribution and hospitality while I was researching in Scotland; Gordon Irving for his contacts north of the border, which included Jimmy Shand, Jack Sinclair and Jim Macleod; Peter Prichard; Alec Myles; Bernard Bresslaw; Norman Vaughan; Jack Douglas; Frankie Howerd; Richard Afton; the Grand Order of Water Rats; Liza Minelli; the Edinburgh Room of the George IV Library; Danny Freidman of the Theatre Museum and the V & A Museum; Eric Merriman; Bunty Gordon; Norman Wisdom; John Counsell of the Theatre Royal Windsor for giving me so much of his time; Sammy Davis Jr; Victor Borge; Lionel Blair; Bruce Trent; *TV Times* picture library; Doug Mackenzie for making such a marvellous job in reproducing some of the memorabilia; the Hulton Picture Library; actor William Moore and his wife Mollie Sugden; my wife Marion for her help when reading the first draft; Geraldine Guthrie for typing the manuscript.

My sincere appreciation goes to Jean Snoad, who did some of the valuable early research. Jean's initial enthusiasm was most helpful to me. I must apologise to all the hundreds of artistes who have appeared in royal performances that space has not allowed me to mention. Their contributions have nevertheless given me an overall guide to the remarkable co-operation between the theatre and the monarchy, who in their turn have helped in the continued growth of entertainment, and given me the opportunity to write this book.

INDEX

Back Cover: Programme, 1849. Courtesy of Theatre Museum